Growing up in
THE SECOND WORLD WAR

Nance Lui Fyson

Batsford Academic and Educational Limited London

© Nance Lui Fyson 1981
First published 1981
This edition published 1982

ISBN 0 7134 3575 5

Printed by R J Acford, Chichester, Sussex
for the Publishers Batsford Academic and
Educational Ltd,
4 Fitzhardinge Street, London W1H 0AH

Frontispiece: **An evacuee is kissed goodbye at the
station**

Acknowledgment

The Author and Publishers thank the following for
their kind permission to reproduce copyright
illustrations: BBC Hulton Picture Library for the
frontispiece and figs 1, 2, 3, 4, 8, 11, 12, 13, 14, 18,
20, 22, 24, 35, 39, 40, 46, 50, 51, 55, 56, 58, 60;
Fox Photos Ltd for figs 5, 7, 10, 15, 16, 17, 19, 21,
27, 29, 36, 37, 41, 42, 47, 49, 52, 53, 57, 59; the
Imperial War Museum for figs 6, 9, 23, 25, 26, 28,
30, 31, 32, 33, 34, 38, 43, 44, 45, 48, 54.

Contents

The Illustrations

2 Bombings and Shelters

My mum said, if you hear a siren run for home. I was scared and ran down this empty road as though I was personally under attack. I must have been about four.

Adrian Walker (b. 1938) and other 1940's children knew all too well about bombings and shelters.

Shelters

In November 1938 the "Anderson shelter" began. This was a shell of corrugated steel sheeting. Put 4 feet (1.2 metres) into the ground, it had over 15 inches (38 centimetres) of earth piled up over the curved roof. Water seeped in and had to be bailed out. Some 2¼ million of these shelters were put up in people's gardens for free. Only about a thousand people whose income was more than £250 a year had to pay — about £6 to £10. The Anderson shelters proved to be a very good protection for up to six people — but also a most uncomfortable way to spend a night.

Night after night we got out of bed. Everything was ready to take down. We waited there until the all-clear. I was always frightened of being trapped. (John Conder, b. 1935)

It was so cramped you really didn't sleep. I thought in the morning "oh, how will I ever go to work?" It was a horrible

3   London's first night air raid, 1940. The "Anderson shelter" looks battered but stood up well. John Conder (b. 1935): "We had nite lights floating in saucers of water. There were bunks on each side. You climbed in down the hole. Beetles crawled up the ceiling and fell on you."
▼

4   1940. Children asleep in a London Underground station shelter. The Holborn-Aldwych branch line was used just for sheltering. Children there slept in hammocks slung between the rails — on tracks where trains normally ran.
▼

feeling. And yet you didn't stay away from work because there'd been a blitz. (Phyllis Bradley, b. 1925)

Many city dwellers had no garden into which an Anderson shelter could be put. Surface communal street shelters for up to fifty people were hastily erected. (Thousands of shelters built in 1940 were unsafely bonded with lime only and had to be rebuilt.) These dark, damp shelters had just wooden benches against the walls. Sometimes children and adults spent as much as fourteen hours there — with no sanitation facilities. But despite the sounds of exploding bombs outside, people made the best of it. Children joined in the singing, or watched as card games were played, and tea flasks passed

around.

Trench shelters were cut into parks. They were liable to flood, but still more popular than the brick surface shelters.

London Underground shelters

The government resisted opening London's Underground Tube stations as shelters, but people gradually began to use these. Near the end of September 1940 some 177,000 people were sleeping in the Tube. A few hundred stayed down there for weeks at a time. These were mostly people who had lost their homes.

Children took bedding and arrived early at the Tube to save a place for the family. Parents later brought more bedding. A white line was drawn 2.4 metres from the edge of the platform. Children had to stay behind this, leaving room for travellers. After 7.30 in the evening children and their families spread up to within 1.2 metres of the edge of the platform. Late arrivers made do on stairs, passages, even on the lines, once the current was cut off for the night.

5   Tilbury Shelter in London's East End, 1941. Children were kept amused, painting on the walls. The shelter was a complex of cellars, arches and vaults under the railway. It was overcrowded and famous for being wild and noisy. Children slept in the noise if they could.

We used to go at about 9 o'clock. You really couldn't sleep until the last train had gone. You were woken up with the most horrendous noise of the first train coming through in the morning. We just didn't get enough sleep. My brother (aged nine) was caned for falling asleep in class. (Harriet Ward, b. 1930)

Conditions in the Tube stations were especially dirty and disorganized early on in the war, before lavatories and other necessary facilities were provided. "It was really very scruffy," remarks Harriet Ward. Supplies of buns, pies, and sandwiches were also eventually organized by the Salvation Army and the WVS (Women's Voluntary Service).

Children were not entirely safe in the Underground. Among the disasters were the deaths of 111 people at Bank Station in 1941. The worst was at Balham in 1940: 64 people were killed and about 550 injured. Sewers and water mains burst and water filled the dark, crowded station.

Children found themselves in other city shelters as well. One, called "Mickey's Shelter", was below the overground railway arches at Stepney in London. The heat was hardly bearable. Profits from the canteen allowed free milk for the children.

Sheltering at home

In November 1940, in central London, about 9% of the people slept in public shelters, 4% in the Underground, and 27%

6 Test explosion on an indoor home "Morrison shelter", first produced in 1940. The steel plate on top was used as a table (even for table tennis). At night, children and their families slept underneath. Over ½ million had been distributed by the end of 1941, free to those earning less than £350 a year.

7 1939. An astonished baby watches as London housewives white-wash the kerbstones and lamppost. Bold white stripes were painted around trees, signposts — anything likely to be a danger in the blacked-out streets. In the country some cows wore white lines in case they strayed onto a road!

in Anderson shelters. The other 60% were either working, or sleeping at home — in ground-floor rooms, in cupboards, or under the stairs. Some just took a chance and slept in their own bed. Harriet Ward (b. 1930) sometimes took shelter under the kitchen table:

> I was lying petrified on the floor under the table when a bomb fell nearby. I could feel the ground heave under me, which was quite frightening.

Many people preferred to stay at home rather than go to a public shelter. Some reinforced their cellars and built blast walls for extra protection. In one Manchester house a small Wendy house of sheet steel was built. Children slept on hammocks inside this. The room outside was full of sandbags, leaving a narrow path. When the bombs fell, adults crept through into the small space below the sleeping children.

Children had some narrow escapes. In 1940 the *Daily Mirror* told the story of a family in a south-west town, who used to drag a wooden box to one side of the bed and some chairs to the other. The two children crawled underneath with their parents and grandmother. When a bomb blew away half the side of the room, large stones fell on the bed — but the family was unhurt. In a town in the south-east a young mother was caught in the street during a raid. She quickly stuffed her baby in a dustbin for safety. And the *News Chronicle* recorded how another mother covered her baby's cot with the fireguard to form a roof. When a flying-bomb hit the house, in 1944, heavy pieces of plaster fell on the guard — but the baby stayed safe.

The blackout

The "blackout" was meant to make it harder for German bombers to identify their position over Britain. Windows (of factories, homes, etc) had to be covered when inside lights were on. Lighting on streets in the evening and at night was very limited. Car headlights were masked, so that only a dim light showed. In the dark streets people carried torches and could light matches — but it was still dangerous and difficult to move about. (Regulations were relaxed somewhat in September 1944, to allow for a "dim-out" in some places.) Children often helped at home with the daily job of covering windows before lights could go on in the evening.

> My father made some black screens to fit the windows. Then you had curtains over them. There wasn't a chink of light. (John Conder, b. 1935)

> We had this wooden frame with blackout material on it. Push it on the window at night. Took it down in the day. When they got blown down you had to make more.
> Then you had sticky brown paper across the glass. Everybody had crosses of this on their windows at home, to try to save them being blown out by all the explosions — but we still didn't end up with much glass. (John Rodgers, b. 1929)

Shop windows too were often being blown out. Signs went up: "Blast!" or "More open than usual". Phyllis Bradley (b. 1925):

> There were shop window dummies lying about. At first you thought it was dead bodies.

8 1940. Children searched the bomb sites for bits of shrapnel, fins of bombs, bits of shell. These were collected and traded. John Conder (b. 1935): "You'd value things particularly if they had a number on them. We were warned that butterfly bombs were prettily painted so children would pick them up. I never saw any. Spent ages looking . . .".

German planes

In contrast to the dark on the ground, were the searchlights directed up into the sky:

> The searchlights crossed the sky looking for planes. Once they had one, all lights were on it, passed from one to another. (John Conder, b. 1935)

Children saw planes shot down:

> I saw an aircraft crash into our local greengrocer, its tail sticking out with the flames. The man bailed out. (John Conder)

Stranger things were seen to fall, like thin strips of foil — dropped by the Germans to try to confuse British radio-location of planes. Colin Ward (b. 1924) remembers "silvery stuff dropped from the sky, strips 9 inches by ¾ [23 x 1.9 cm]". And it was not only bombs that children were trying to avoid:

> German fighters used to just splatter the streets with bloomin' tracer bullets. We used to run, run as fast as you could up the alleys and that. Get out of the way. (John Rodgers, b. 1929)

Bombings and the Blitz

The first bombing attack on Britain's mainland was in May 1940. The later bombings of British *cities* began rather by mistake. Hitler had ordered his pilots *not* to bomb London, but two mistakenly did drop bombs on the capital on the night of 24 August 1940. The next morning Britain's Bomber Command had orders to bomb Berlin. Targets had become civilian as well as military.

Children watched the "Battle of Britain" in the skies overhead in the months of August to October 1940. Machine guns clattered as British fighters clashed with German bombers. On 15 August there were some 1,790 enemy aeroplanes over southeast England.

The "Blitz" started with 300 German bombers on the night of 7 September 1940 and lasted for nine months, until 10 May 1941. The Germans then turned their attention towards Russia. London, Liverpool, Hull, Plymouth, Bristol, Southampton, Portsmouth, Glasgow had been among the places hit. Towns such as Canterbury, Exeter, Norwich, and Bath were also raided. On 29 December 1940 some 1,400 fires were raging in the City of London. It was the second Great Fire of London. Luckily, St Paul's Cathedral was not destroyed. At first, it was just the East End in London that was hit. This created bad feeling. But even Buckingham Palace was eventually hit a few times before the Blitz was over.

Joe C. of Wapping in East London was a nine-year-old in a family bombed *five times* (*Daily Herald*, 1940). The family was first bombed while they were on the stairs at home. In the next raid their house was destroyed while they were in a shelter. Bombs fell near them a third time in the street. Another bomb fell on them when they reached their new home. The next night, when they had moved again — they were bombed once more!

John Rodgers (b. 1929) remembers:

We had incendiary bombs on the roof one night. Lucky one of my brothers was on leave. (My father was in the army and my two brothers were in the navy. There was only me, my mother and sister at home.) My brother got up in the loft and we threw the bombs out.

Children also became used to the UXBs — the "unexploded bombs". About 10% of bombs dropped on London were duds. But some had delayed-action fuses. All had to be treated as if they might explode. Houses had to be left and roads closed while these were defused.

Children were constantly warned about the dangers of playing with objects they might find. Two Luton boys aged eleven

9 A North London shelter. The overflow of children and adults from the crowded main shelter slept on benches in this boiler room, by the ashes.

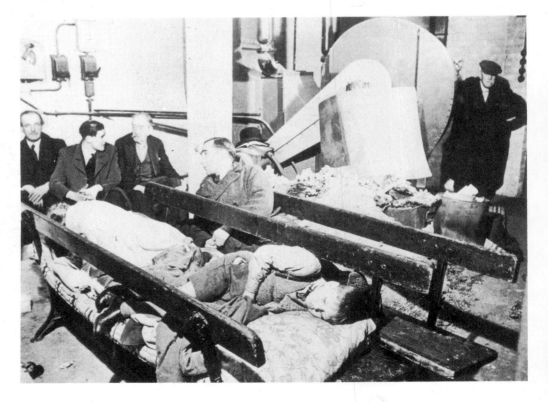

and twelve had a lucky escape when they took home a fully charged five-centimetre-high explosive mortar bomb (*Evening Standard*, 1943). The boys actually knocked out the detonator with a pointed file. Officers later said it was "a chance in a thousand that it did not explode."

But children were among the many people hurt in the bombings. More than two thirds of the approximately 60,000 civilians killed throughout the war died in the bombings of 1940 and 1941 and about a half were in London. Many more people (over 86,000) were seriously injured and put in hospital. Over 150,000 more people had lesser injuries. (The total loss of life in the armed forces was about 264,000.)

Trekking

Coventry was the target of a terrible raid in November 1940. Some 50,000 homes, 500 shops and the historic cathedral were destroyed. The next morning refugees left the city on foot, taking with them what they could. Some children slept with their families against hedgerows. This "trekking", (homeless people leaving the cities) was a familiar sight during the Blitz. Many trekked out of cities in the evening, slept where they could, and returned in the morning.

In spring 1941 Belfast was bombed several times. A hundred thousand trekkers (called "ditchers" in Northern Ireland) left for the countryside.

Censorship

Children were not allowed to talk or write about the bombings they had seen. Harriet Ward (b. 1930):

A few bombs dropped around us in Cornwall. We rushed down to have a look at the craters. I wrote an account of this in detail to my sister in America. The letter got sent back, censored.

(Villages and country areas had a share of the bombings as well.)

10   1941. A mobile shower/bath unit was sent round blitzed areas, providing free baths for bombed-out families. The explosions and collapsing buildings threw up tremendous dust and dirt.

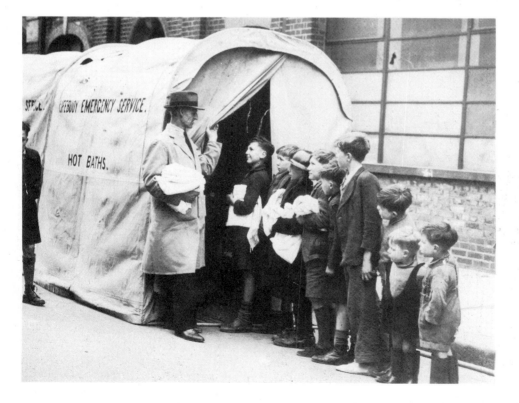

After the Blitz — flying-bombs

Spring 1942 began a year of "tip and run" raids across Britain, with bombs scattered widely. 1943 was the quietest year of the war for air raids, but still thousands of people slept in the London Underground, where conditions had become somewhat better.

In early 1944 there was another large attack on London. On 12 June the V1 "flying-bombs" appeared. Also known as "buzz bombs" or "doodlebugs", some 8,000 of them caused much damage until mid-August. One baby was born in a hospital as it was hit by a flying-bomb (*Evening News*, 1944).

By 1944 many children who had been sent away from the cities early in the war had returned home. An article in the *Daily Herald* described the scene when a flying-bomb hit a road in southern England. A little girl pushed a bent pram through the wreckage. She whispered to the men digging in the ruins of a smashed house. They brought out a teddy bear, torn and slashed, and a doll with its face punched with holes. Injured children wandered about. Five children had been killed. The article was meant to remind people that evacuated children should not yet return.

The *Daily Mirror* in September 1944 showed an eleven-year-old boy looking at a pile of rubble which had been his home. He had been away for years, but was brought back because people thought it was "all right now". He awoke under a pile of ceiling, tiles, and glass.

John Conder (b. 1935) remembers:

At the time of the V bombs I was being evacuated again. My clothes were all laid out on the bed upstairs. We were to spend the night in the shelter. A bomb landed nearby. I remember shaking and hitting my head. I rushed out and looked up and there was a round cloud of smoke directly overhead. I thought the house had gone but it had just brought the ceilings down. Next morning I had to dig my clothes out.

Over a thousand V2 rockets came over between 8 September 1944 and March 1945, when the bombing of Britain ended.

11 Children and their families shelter in the caves of Dover, 1944. Being nearest to Europe, Dover was the most harassed town in Britain. There were more than 3,000 warnings of bombings and shellings over the war years. 600 people in the area were killed or badly injured.

3 Evacuees

The government urged parents to send children to safety — but evacuation was always voluntary. No one was forced to go. Areas of Britain were declared either "evacuation", "reception", or "neutral". (Some areas, like Plymouth and Bristol, were not labelled high-risk evacuation areas, but were later heavily bombed.) 13 million people had been living in evacuation areas, 18 million in the thought-to-be-safer reception areas, and 14 million in neutral zones. About 4 million people were a priority for evacuation: schoolchildren together with their teachers, pre-school children with their mothers, expectant mothers, and blind adults and cripples.

12   1939. Evacuated children were read to by candle-light in their country homes (by 1943, only a quarter of the farms in England and Wales had electricity). A lot of city children had never even seen the country, or farms, before. It was hard for many children to settle in — but at least they had a whole new range of experiences.

The first evacuation

Evacuees began moving out of cities on 1 September 1939 — two days before war was declared officially. It was thought that war might start with immediate bombings by the Germans — but this was not the case. By 3 September nearly 1½ million people (mostly children) had been moved to reception areas. This was just the official government scheme. By the end of the first few weeks of the war, 2 million other people had evacuated themselves by private arrangement.

The numbers who left evacuation areas varied from place to place. Just over half the schoolchildren in London stayed put. In Liverpool, Newcastle and Manchester over 60% left. In some places, like Sheffield, as few as 15% of schoolchildren went. On average, 47% of schoolchildren in England's evacuation areas did move to safer areas, while in Scotland the average figure was 38%.

Despite preparations, there was confusion and chaos in some reception areas. When children, and others, arrived, some were randomly placed. Sometimes hosts took their pick of the children. Strong lads were wanted by farmers. Girls aged ten to twelve were popular for the help they could give in the home. Small allowances were made to householders who took in evacuees.

Because the expected air attacks did not start, by January 1940 over half of the evacuees had gone back home again. Only about one third of Liverpool and London children stayed in reception areas.

The second evacuation

The decision was taken to evacuate again only once bombing had actually started. The focus was to be on the schoolchildren. (Evacuating mothers with their young

13 June 1940. In one week nearly a hundred thousand London schoolchildren were evacuated, mostly to the West Country. For some, this was their second time. Children here carry their boxed gas masks as well as sandwiches for the trip.

children had been particularly unsuccessful.) In spring 1940, in London, fewer than 10% of schoolchildren were registered for the new evacuation scheme, and only 2% of householders in reception areas offered to accept evacuees. The first experience had put many people off the whole idea. But in September 1940 the second official evacuation did go into effect. About 1¼ million people were moved — many for the second time. (By then billets were also needed for wartime industry workers who had been moved.) This second time, too, evacuees drifted back to the cities, in spite of the dangers.

"Seavacuation"

Children were being sent outside Britain as well. By May 1940 there were offers to take British children to America and the Dominions. CORB, the Children's Overseas Reception Board, was set up. The cost of travel was met by the government, with contributions from the parents depending on what they could afford.

In September 1940 the *Daily Telegraph* reported that some 320 children being "seavacuated" to Canada had been aboard a ship which was torpedoed. All were taken from the ship in lifeboats and returned to Britain. The paper noted how cool and cheerful the children were, singing "Roll out the barrel" as they left the ship, huddled in lifejackets and blankets. But that same month another ship was sunk, losing 73 "seavacuees". The CORB scheme was ended (after 2,500 children had been sent). Another 14,000 were sent privately overseas, more than one third to the USA. American seamen offered to "seavacuate" British children, without taking wages — but only if poor as well as rich children were carried.

14 1942. Small parties of children were still leaving London for the country. Here a teacher puts a label on one of her boys — who looks none too happy about leaving home.

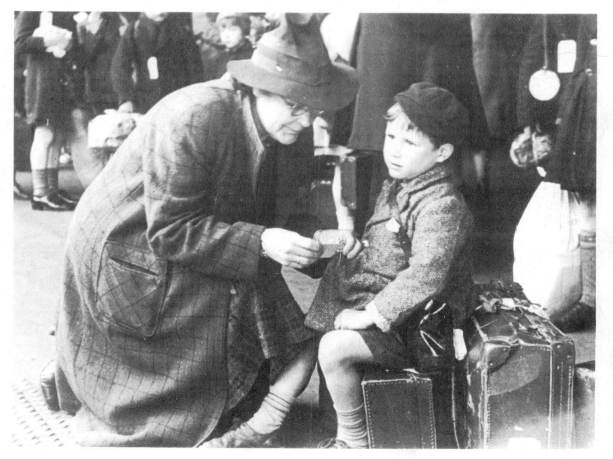

Some experiences of evacuation

John Conder (b. 1935) was an East-End Londoner sent to the West Country:

> The first time I was evacuated in 1940 I went with my brother and mother to a doctor's house. It was snobby. They weren't pleased to have us. We had the servants' quarters as well, which didn't help. We left.
>
> The next time I was evacuated, we didn't stay very long in the first house. My mother made contact with the butcher so we moved in there. The butcher was also a farmer. I used to have the job of collecting the eggs. There were so many animals!

Evacuee children had worries about what was happening at home. John Conder's father was driving trains in the East End, in the Dock area. "He was having a rough time."

1944 evacuations

In February 1941 there were some 1,340,000 people officially evacuated. One year later, after the Blitz, only 738,000 were still in reception areas. But another large wave of evacuation came after the first flying-bomb fell on London in June 1944. The area of the south-east (including London) was known as "buzzbomb alley". And yet, despite the flying-bombs and the V2 rockets which began later in the year, many evacuated children continued to drift home.

Alan Skilton (b. 1934) was evacuated to Oldham in 1944 and found the change very hard:

> I had a certain resentment because the papers always showed the evacuated children in the countryside or seaside. Whereas I found myself in "smokey Oldham" in a house with a paved backyard after being brought up in a suburban house with garden in Enfield. I was so homesick.

He wrote home soon after the journey:

> Dear Mum and Dad,
> On the train journey we saw three aerodromes and one of the aeroplanes was taking off . . . . When we got out of the train at Oldham there were private buses ready for us which took us to a Co-operative place . . . . After that we went to a Sunday school used as a rest centre. There we had mattresses, and two blankets, and a pillar. The boys had a pillar fight. We had our breakfast and dinner at the Co-operative place and then afterwards the people came for us . . . . It is an industrial town, the chief thing is cotton mills . . . .
>
> Before the people came to take us we had another medical . . . . The buses are different colours than ours . . . . They have got trams here . . . . PS We have a kitten called Sandy and there is not any garden.

Alan Skilton arrived at Oldham on a wet evening after that journey. He remembers:

> Our destination was kept secret until we arrived. Being chosen was like being bidded for in a slave market. It was distressing because my friend and I were left towards the end. Two boys together were not the favourite catch.

A slightly later letter home showed his difficulty in settling down:

> Dear Mum and Dad,
> I like the place and the people but I would like to come home. I went to the school today but I didn't like it so much as our school . . . . I amuse myself going to the fields or looking at books. I'm wearing my long socks but I don't want anymore. Was it hot yesterday because it was here. We have no garden to play in. There is a girl living here. I wish I could come home.

15 1941. This evacuee was not able to take her doll's pram with her — so the farmer loaned her a yoke to take her dolls for a walk.

A letter from the woman looking after Alan in Oldham showed how hard it could be for people who took in evacuees:

> Dear Mrs. Skilton
> I am sorry Alan is not settling down . . . .
> he still cries rather a lot . . . . I have done everything possible to make them happy and comfortable . . . but of course they miss their garden . . . .

Another evacuee was Kathleen Rodgers (b. 1933), who was sent from London to Reading for the whole war:

> It was elderly people we were with. They were very good but we were kept under so much. We never played with children, never went in the street. Sundays was Sunday School in the morning, Sunday School in the afternoon, church in the evening. Our parents came to see us when they could. When I came home I could go in and out when I liked.

The end of the war

The number of evacuees by March 1945 was 400,000 and these were mainly from London. Only some 54,000 made use of the official return scheme when the war ended. And so there were still 76,000 evacuees some three months later. Many of these had no homes to go back to. Some children had been abandoned. As the months went on, the number of evacuees was still about 38,000. Local authorities took charge of unclaimed children.

The poorest evacuees

Evacuation did save the lives of some children. It also drew attention to problems of poverty. Some very poor evacuees had never cleaned their teeth, had water from an inside tap, lived with carpets, slept in a bed. Some very poor children arrived actually sewn into their one set of ragged clothes. They had never worn underwear or pyjamas. They were not used to sitting at table, eating with a knife and fork. Some arrived with fleas, headlice, impetigo, scabies. Bed-wetting and lack of toilet training was another problem with 5-10% of evacuees. Some of the very poorest children had not been used to using a toilet at all. (In big city tenements, one lavatory might have had to be shared by four or five large families.) Hosts, especially middle-class or richer families, who took in such evacuated children, were often shocked to learn that such poverty still existed.

Some hostesses complained that evacuees arrived poorly clothed — and yet received generous pocket money from home. Another complaint was that children had been used to going to bed late and at irregular hours. Some children had been used to having just a piece of bread and marg with jam, standing on the doorstep or in the street. Or they were just used to fish and chips. Such children refused green vegetables, soups, salads, which they had never had before. (The poorest city children came from homes where it was difficult to store and prepare such foods.)

The complaints were not all one-way.

Some "foster" homes were far from clean and kind — though most did their best to cope. However, despite all the problems, there were many cases of evacuees and their foster families becoming very closely attached to each other.

16 1941. City children evacuated to a Devon farm found themselves helping with the potato harvest, then given an outside bath with water from a pump. (By 1943 less than half the farms of England and Wales had a supply of piped water.)

4 Refugees

Jewish children from the continent were among the refugees who came to Britain. A World Movement for the Care of Children from Germany had been started in Britain in 1938, and by the time the war began, over 9,000 children (nearly 7,500 Jewish) had arrived on their own. Other children came with just one or both parents. Children with no relations or friends in Britain were maintained by the organization or by local committees.

Coming to Britain undoubtedly saved many children's lives. About 2 million Jewish children died in the persecution on the continent. At least one million of these were deliberately put to death by the Nazis. (Millions more adults — mainly Jews — had been gassed, starved, or otherwise murdered as well by 1945.) But, while the refugee children who came here were grateful for being saved, the move was a hard one. Children faced leaving their parents, their homes, coming to a strange country with a language and customs which they did not know. Some parents pretended that they would be following soon — but they must have realized how impossible this would become. Many children simply never saw their families again.

Jewish friends used to hear until 1940 or 41 from relief organizations and then just didn't hear anything until after the war of what had happened to their relations. (Colin Ward, b. 1924)

Karen Gershon was one child who came. Her later book collection of the experiences of the Jewish refugees (*We Came as Children*) gives much detail about how these children felt and the difficulties they encountered. They arrived with the one suitcase they had each been allowed. Some remember crossing the German border with relief that they no longer had to look over their shoulders with fear. But many children were at first very unhappy, feeling lost, and missing their families.

Reception centres

Once in England, some children were taken to Dovercourt — a summer holiday camp — where they slept in small cabins. The winter was bitterly cold. The children slept fully clothed, even wearing scarves and gloves. But at least one child thought: whatever the hardships, better this than being in Germany. Some children went to another camp near Lowestoft. Some spent nights sleeping on the ballroom floor of a big hotel.

In the camps the children were taught English, and about Britain. Some of them then went on to stay in hostels. But efforts were made to place children in families where possible.

Alien camps

One child, aged ten, could hardly believe how "normal" life was in England — that, as Jews, they could go into a shop, along the street, or on a bus without fearing attacks and insults. But in 1940 many German Jewish refugees in Britain were interned as "enemy aliens" and put into camps. This included many German Jewish teenage refugees who could hardly believe that they were suspect. Some were sent to Australia.

Mixed experiences

Charles Hannam (b. 1926 in Essen, Germany) came to England in 1939 at the age of thirteen. He "hated being a refugee and not belonging anywhere". As an alien, he could not join the Home Guard and had to report regularly to the police. He later joined the British army in 1944 and went on to Cambridge University in 1948.

The experiences of the young Jewish refugees were mixed. Some found themselves thought of as spies. And yet, as Jews, they were as against the Nazis as their English friends. More than a thousand young Jewish refugees became members of the British forces, and about thirty died.

Some refugee children were laughed at because of their broken English and foreign ways. But others thought English children kind and helpful. It was a hard time for many refugees. One remembers being in three homes and three schools within twelve months.

Ruth Stanley (b. 1930) was not a refugee but born in Liverpool into a religious Jewish family. She remembers her parents talking about Jewish lives being threatened just before the war ("they discussed it endlessly"):

My family had an extra, deeper commitment to the war.

17 1939. German Jewish children at the refugee children's camp at Dovercourt receive stamps for letters they wrote home to Europe. Many European Jewish children had not the good fortune to escape. Many governments (including Britain's) could have helped far more. The liner *St Louis* in 1939 was not unusual. Nine hundred German Jewish refugees spent weeks sailing to find a country that would take them in.

5 Foreign Soldiers and Prisoners of War

By late spring 1944 there were nearly 1½ million Allied, Dominion and colonial troops in Britain. The build-up was especially heavy before D-Day (6 June 1944), when 156,000 troops crossed the Channel and landed in France. John Rodgers (b. 1929):

We used to get mixed up running up and down the road with the French sailors, and the Yanks and everybody else having brawls in the pubs and that.

American GIs

The most frequently seen foreign soldiers were the American GIs (GI because of their equipment stamped "Government Issue"). The GIs had all sorts of goods which were hard to find in Britain — razor blades, candies, nylon stockings. GIs were generous to British children. John Conder (b. 1935):

They spoke so differently. And there were black ones as well and they had smart uniforms. And we'd heard they'd got plenty of food and money. Everyone was terribly jealous of them.

The American soldiers were much better paid and better dressed than their English equivalents.

GIs made good use of such treasures as stockings, nail varnish, and cigarettes in chatting up British girls. Phyllis Bradley (b. 1925):

We were always told to beware of the GIs. Because they couldn't dance I didn't ever bother. I enjoyed meeting them. But you never took them really seriously.

But many British girls, about 50,000, did become their brides.

Black GIs were treated badly by white GIs, which upset the British. British girls happily danced with black GIs, and this angered white American soldiers. Children saw local pubs filled with black and white GIs and the fights that broke out between them.

POWs

Besides foreign soldiers, children in Britain saw foreign prisoners of war who were made to work here (some 130,000 Italians and 90,000 Germans).

The POWs were laying drains. They used to like talking to kids. The guards seemed very relaxed. The prisoners wore these uniforms with patches sewn in so they couldn't run off easily. (Adrian Walker, b. 1938).

Young people also saw their own forces returning from sometimes very harsh treatment abroad.

One boy came home after being a prisoner of war with the Japanese. He had changed completely. We nicknamed him "the skeleton". (Phyllis Bradley, b. 1925)

The Channel Islands

The only part of Britain ever occupied by

German soldiers were the Channel Islands (from the summer of 1940 until 1945). Some children had been evacuated from there before the Germans took over, but many remained. German was made compulsory in the schools. Some of the children were among the 2,000 people deported to Germany for internment in camps. Children remaining on the Islands saw thousands of slave workers brought from Europe, clothed in rags, and with rags tied round their feet.

18 Over two hundred English children (orphans and other victims of the Blitz) enjoy a party given for them by the US Army Air Forces at headquarters, 1942. American forces were "super people" to English children. John Conder (b. 1935): "We used to pester the lives out of them. They used to give you things. We'd say 'Got any gum, chum?'."

6 Schools and Education

We lost a lot of schooling. You wouldn't go to school for odd weeks because of the bombings and that. Then there was no heating or something. You were in one day and out another. When the air raids went you were down the bloomin' shelter.

That was the case for John Rodgers (b. 1929) who stayed in London. And for children who were evacuated, there were many upsets as well.

When the war started, many schools in high-risk areas were closed at first. But a lot of children were not sent away from these areas. The government was not willing to force parents to evacuate children, and so the re-opening of some schools became necessary. As many schools as possible

19   1939. Schools in the New Malden area were closed because of the evacuation. Classes for those children left were held in private houses. Teachers visited small groups of children for about 1½ hours each day, and left them homework. In January 1940 about one quarter of schoolchildren in evacuated areas were having only Home Tuition and another quarter (430,000 children) were having no schooling at all.

were made splinter- and shrapnel-proof. Sometimes the children had to go to school in shifts.

Air raid drills were part of the curriculum. One junior school in Scunthorpe boasted in 1939 that the children could reach the shelters in the playing fields in a little over two minutes. Children wore their gas masks while carrying out the drill.

Evacuated children found themselves having lessons in whatever halls or rooms could be found. Nearly one hundred girls evacuated from Newcastle spent four and a half years at school at Alnwick Castle.

Some evacuated schools were kept together. Some were added to village schools, with overcrowding the result. Adrian Walker (b. 1938):

There was a shortage of space. A lot of evacuee kids had swollen the population. They were known as "vacs". We were taught in the church hall across the road as well. There were two classes simultaneously, just screens between, which we

used to try to knock over. They used to do singing lessons in one class and they'd be trying to do history in the other.

Even before the war, one third of all classes in elementary schools had over forty pupils, and 100,000 children were in classes of over fifty. The situation was as bad or worse in many areas during the war because of the shortage of teachers and buildings. Public schools had the advantage of about one teacher for every sixteen pupils, while the average for state secondary schools was one to twenty-five or thirty pupils. Some school buildings were taken over for war use, including two thirds of London's schools and 60% in Manchester.

20 1940. Pupils of Cheltenham College leave Shrewsbury School on their way home to town billets. White sweaters were to help them be seen in the blackout. The two schools had to share facilities. Such doubling up, as well as shifts for schooling, added to all the disruptions of education during the war.

Memories of school in wartime

The changes of schools and disruption of lessons were hard for many evacuees. John Conder (b. 1935):

> The village school was so different from a town school. It was one hall, two or three classes in different parts of this one room, all age children together. I made a terrible bloomer the first day. The teacher said "fill the sheet of paper with the letter 'a'." I just got one big one in, quite quickly. I looked round to see why the others were taking so much time. They were doing lines of small letters.

Many country schools had a Babies' Room for under-sevens, with one teacher. Another teacher had the Big Room for children seven to fourteen.

Adrian Walker (b. 1938) remembers:

> There were inkwells in the desk and those awful wooden pens. They used to splat everywhere. We used to call proper writing "double-writing" because it was joined up.

Pens, like many other things, were made to a wartime "utility" standard. From May 1942 pencils, too, of only a certain type and size were made.

Because so many men were away at war, many children were being taught by older teachers who had retired.

> We were taught by older women, and just a few older men. Things then got tough. All these young guys came back from the war about 1945, 46 and they weren't going to take any nonsense. (Adrian Walker)

Discipline in schools varied:

> They hit us on the hands with rulers, clipped us round the ear. (Adrian Walker)

Alan Skilton (b. 1934) evacuated to Oldham, Lancs. in 1944:

> In school there the leather strap was used quite freely on boys and girls for bad work whereas in Enfield only the cane was used, for real delinquents.

21 South-west London, 1940. Some schools were having just one school session from 9.30 am to 2.00 pm (with a short lunch-break) so that children would not be on the streets during mid-day air raids.

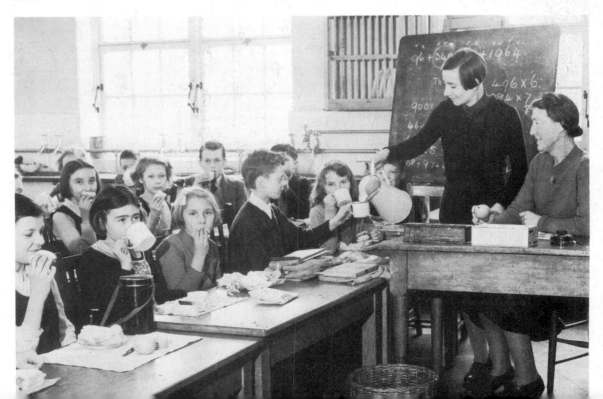

Many country schools were still lit by gas, with gas stoves for warmth.

We had these pot-bellied stoves. We used to try to flick rubbers on the top. (Adrian Walker)

Schools and the war effort

Some boys' schools did war work in their metalwork classes. If they had any ground, schools made their own vegetable gardens. One Inner London school produced masses of potatoes and other vegetables on derelict land. School hobby clubs were very practical (pig-keeping, mending clothes, repairing shoes, etc). Many children missed school to help with farming.

The education system

90% of children in England and Wales were within the state system of education. Since the First World War about five sixths of these stayed until the age of fourteen in elementary schools. (The school-leaving age had been raised to fourteen in 1918.) One sixth went from the age of eleven to either technical schools or grammar schools.

The "special place" examination to go to a grammar school was sat at age eleven. Those few children who went to a secondary school took a "School Certificate" exam at sixteen. A "Higher School Certificate" could be taken at eighteen, to gain a university or college place. (By 1944 the universities had one quarter fewer students and one third fewer teachers than before the war. Department research was largely directed to the war effort.) All the disruptions of education made exam-taking much harder. One lot of evacuees, taking the Higher School Certificate in 1940, had to write their papers after they had spent a night up guarding a railway tunnel.

The Butler Act of 1944 made a number of important changes to education. It said that every child should receive some kind of secondary education. (This had been recommended as far back as 1926 by one of the Hadow Reports — but only some local authorities had been setting up "central", "senior", or "modern" schools in addition to the grammar schools.) Before the Butler Act, Local Education Authorities were only required by law to provide elementary education for children. Now, a selection

22 Besides ordinary gas masks, there were special children's masks that were bright red with a beak in front. (For babies there were air-tight chambers into which filtered air was pumped by hand bellows.) Adrian Walker (b. 1938): "We used to have to practise wearing our masks at school. They were horrible, rubbery, nasty things." Gas attacks were much feared at the start of the war — but these never occurred. Gradually, people carried their masks less and less.

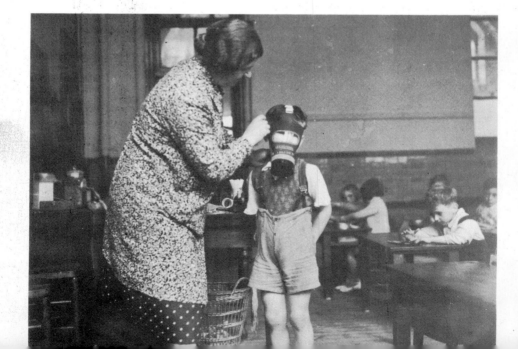

▲

23 Schools helped the war effort in many ways, including by collecting salvage. Signs on the wall of this room refer to "Our Allies the Colonies". Signs in other classrooms reminded children to "Help a Prisoner of War" and that "Careless Talk Costs Lives. Be like Dad, Keep Mum."

24 1943. A school in London where thirty children ▶ and four teachers were killed during a daylight raid. About one fifth of Britain's schools were damaged by bombs during the war. Some children in Cambridge had the surprise of a German bomber plane landing suddenly in the school yard!

test (the "eleven-plus") was set up to direct every child at age eleven into either grammar school, junior technical school, or secondary modern school. Also, for the first time, schools were required to give some religious instruction.

The school-leaving age was to have been raised to fifteen in September 1939 (Education Act of 1936), then in 1945 — and it finally happened in 1947.

7 Work, and Helping the War Effort

Fears of invasion in 1940 prompted a great scare about a Fifth Column, spies in Britain. Children and adults were urged by Ministry of Information advertisements to keep information to themselves. "Careless Talk Costs Lives" was the slogan. Dangerous citizens were people like "Miss Leaky Mouth". John Conder (b. 1935):

> There were constant warnings "Walls have ears", "Spies are everywhere". . . . A little Irishman asked me the way to Ford's factory which was nearby. I expect he wanted a job there. I sent him in the opposite direction.

25 Collecting salvage in Suffolk. The children have just driven in a pony cart filled with waste paper. In the depot, papers, bottles, rags, etc, were all sorted. A central depot collected materials about once a month to sell to wholesale dealers.
▼

A ditty taught to schoolchildren was: "If anyone stops me to ask the way, all I must answer is 'I can't say'."

Children also helped with scattering junk (old bedsteads, etc) on empty areas of ground where German planes might have been able to land. "Pill-box" defences and tank-traps were erected near major roads.

Collecting salvage

The Ministry of Supply announced in July 1940 that collecting salvage was to be compulsory. Especially needed were waste paper and cardboard, scrap metal, and household bones. Kitchen waste was collected and processed for pigs. Other items recycled were tins, gramophone records, films, rags, jars and bottles.

Children were very active in the collecting. One mother returned home to find that her little girl had turned in every utensil

they had! Some Ilford boys evacuated to Wales made a weekend house-to-house collection. They piled hundreds of pots and pans in the local square. Much of this turned out to be wasted effort, as the metal was not re-usable — but about 5 million tons of metal were salvaged during the war and re-used. From 1940, wrought-iron railings were taken down from around many town squares, parks, cemeteries — letting children into areas which they had been kept out of before. Large bins were placed on streets (inside some householders' front gardens) for bone and paper.

Collectors and salvage wardens wore a brown circle labelled with an "S". Schoolchildren collectors were known as "COGS". Their anthem was: "There'll always be a dustbin". By 1943 some 3 million tons of paper had been collected and about half the paper used in Britain was being recycled. 56 million books had been handed in for pulping and 50 million of these were recycled. For book collection, children could earn a coloured badge and move from being a "private" to a "sergeant" to a "general".

National Savings

By March 1943 the British had lent over £5,000 million to the government in the National Savings Campaign. By then individuals were saving an average of 25% of their after-tax incomes — compared to less than 6% before the war. John Conder (b. 1935):

> You used to buy savings stamps and stick them on these bombs in the library and they'd be delivered to Hitler for you.

◄ 26 There were some 300,000 National Savings groups in the country. Schools made posters. People felt that they were helping to "buy" military equipment. But the main aim was to keep down inflation. There was much more money about than goods on which to spend it.

Advertisements for National Savings showed a smiling boy squashing the "squanderbug" in his stamp book.

> The "squanderbug" was a cartoon evil, nasty looking creature — that was squandering and wasting. (John Conder)

Regular groups (at work, schools, in streets, etc) also saved and held "savings drives" — such as "Wings for Victory" week. Children joined in the collecting. Parades and displays made the weeks festive occasions. Groups looked at "price lists" of items issued by the government and chose how to "spend" what they had collected. The favourite "purchase" was to loan the government £5,000 for a Spitfire aeroplane.

The forces

Children were not allowed to fight in the war. But a few mistakes were made. A newspaper report in 1942 told of a boy of ten being called up. His mother went with him to the National Service Office to explain the error. However, teenagers officially too young for the forces found themselves very close to the action. Sixteen-year-old cadets, crack rifle shots, were guarding London defences. Albert Barnes was a fourteen-year-old galley boy on a tugboat rescuing men at the Dunkirk evacuation of 1940. (Over 225,000 British soldiers — and another 113,000 other troops — were brought back across the Channel, some in small civilian boats.) John Atkins was a fifteen-year-old barge-hand who was fatally wounded in the famous rescue.

Conscription was extended downwards to boys of age eighteen and upwards to men aged fifty-one at the end of 1941. A conscript to the armed forces could, in theory, choose between the Royal Navy, the Royal Air Force, or the Army (the least popular). Boys of fourteen-plus could join cadet forces (the Sea Cadet Corps, the Air Training

Corps, or the Army Cadet Force) and volunteer for the adult service just before the age of eighteen. (This improved their chances of getting into the service of their choice.) Boys took part in cadet forces along with their regular day work.

In December 1941 there was a "Registration of Boys and Girls Order" on all sixteen- and seventeen-year-olds. This was to encourage more young people to join a youth club or organization that was doing some national service.

Women were conscripted for the first time during the Second World War. (Britain was the only country doing this.) At first, it was only unmarried women aged twenty to thirty, but this was later extended upwards and downwards.

A list of "reserved occupations", which meant that people in certain jobs were not taken for service, was ended in 1940.

27 1940. Earls Court Stadium became a factory for making tents and haversacks for the forces. Teenage boys coiled and spliced ropes for the tents.

"Bevin Boys"

The shortage of miners prompted Ernest Bevin, then Minister of Labour, to direct youths to work in the mines as part of their National Service. From the end of 1943, 10% of boys reaching military service age were chosen as "Bevin Boys" by ballot. Some 45,000 boys, coming from all social classes, eventually found themselves in this unpopular service.

The Home Guard

A radio broadcast in May 1940 asked for recruits and within a few days nearly a quarter of a million men had signed up for the "Local Defence Volunteers". The age limits were officially seventeen to sixty-five but many older and younger joined. Renamed the "Home Guard", this was largely a volunteer force of young lads, men unable to join the forces for health reasons, and men too old for the services. Manning anti-aircraft guns and bomb disposal were two of the tasks they took on. Over a thousand men died in the course of Home Guard duties.

Henry Ricketts (b. 1923) was in the Home Guard from the beginning until it ended in 1944. As well as doing his office job, he was on Home Guard duty from 8 o'clock at night until 6 in the morning, one day in four.

Some nights you'd get no sleep at all. Other nights you might get a couple of hours.

He recalls that the "young lads and old chaps got on well":

In them days, there was a far different feeling between the younger generation and the older generation. The younger generation had more respect. In spite of the bad nights we had, I'd like to see now the same sort of companionship. Everybody was far more friendly.

Fire-watching

Henry Ricketts also did fire-watching duty some nights at the office where he worked. Fire-watching was compulsory in large factories from September 1940, and in small shops and offices as well by the end of the year. Members of staff took it in turn to watch, when the building was closed for the night. Small fires started by incendiary bombs could be put out quickly if caught in time.

War work

Two thirds of males and females aged fourteen to sixty-five were doing full-time war work by 1943. Many were doing more jobs than one. And many more who could not do full-time work were working part-time. Women working less than 55 hours a week and men working less than 60 had to put in an extra 48 hours a month in the Civil Defence, fire-watching, or with the Home Guard. There were also millions of jobs being done by voluntary, unpaid workers. By June 1944, 22% of Britain's labour force were in the services and 33% doing war work as civilians.

An end to unemployment

In the depression years of the 1930s young people leaving school had joined the large numbers of adults unable to find work. Unemployment was especially high in the north of England, Scotland and Wales. (By 1937 the worst was over and yet one sixth of the Scottish and one quarter of the Welsh labour force were still without jobs.) A transfer scheme had been set up so that boys and girls could go to jobs in other parts of the country. But while thousands of teenagers did this, it was never liked and the drift home was speeded up by the coming of war.

Early in the war youth unemployment continued and even went up in some areas. But as war production grew, and many adult workers were drawn into the services, the demand for boys and girls grew. Their unemployment quickly dropped from 1941 on. Phyllis Bradley (b. 1925):

I started by making up the army uniforms. It was all so exciting.

Ministry of Labour figures showed the change in the kind of jobs that boys and girls aged fourteen to seventeen were doing over the years 1938-45. The number of boys working in agriculture increased, as did the number of boys in railway service. The number of boys in coal mining decreased by more than half. More boys were being employed in the aircraft industry, while in general engineering there was a dramatic increase in boy employees until 1942 and '43, though by 1945 numbers had fallen back to less than before the war. With girls, there were nearly three times as many working in general engineering by 1943 than in 1938, but their number fell considerably by 1945.

Early in the war boys and girls were not

told to do specific jobs. But the Essential Work Order passed in 1941 meant that juveniles too could be directed towards work that was part of the war effort.

Boys in building

The building industry suffered a sharp decrease in number of boys — which increased again only in 1945. Before the war boys working in the building industry were being trained as apprentices. But as the war went on, they were just filling in the shortage of adult workers. Boys helped erect buildings and clear bomb debris. Boys of fifteen, sixteen and seventeen were getting little instruction — but earning high wages. Many shared hostels with adult men. The industry and government worried about this. In late 1941 a scale limited youth wage rates. In 1942 the hours were limited to 48 a week for the under sixteens and to 54 for boys of sixteen and seventeen. Boys under sixteen

were then stopped from working on demolition and clearance work and on contracts where they would have to live in camps.

Other jobs for young people

Young people did all sorts of jobs. John Rodgers (b. 1929) delivered newspapers throughout the war for a small wage. He also received the perk each week of a couple of cigarettes or a couple of sweets (without having to use a coupon). Colin Ward (b. 1924):

> At fifteen I was working for a man who put up air-raid shelters for the local council. We dug the holes.

Because of labour shortages, young people were doing a lot of jobs which they did not usually do. In 1943 a chief constable reported his worry at the increasing number of boys and girls as young as fifteen and sixteen employed in pubs serving drinks.

John Rodgers (b. 1929):

> We all used to have to help, however old you were. Even the toddlers used to fill sandbags to put round the air raid shelter.

28 Teenage girls at work in a textile mill. Only about half as many girls aged fourteen to seventeen worked in textiles by 1945 as had been in the industry in 1938. The number of girls in tailoring and dressmaking also declined.

29 1942. Worthing children formed a "Black-out Corps" to help paint the windows of large premises. Here two girls help black-out a local hospital.

Hours of work

When the war started, there was no law limiting hours of work for adult men — but there was for women and young people. As higher production was needed during the war, the rules set down in the Factories Act 1937 were relaxed for government work. Women and boys over sixteen were thus allowed to work at night, and young people under sixteen were allowed by Emergency Order to work up to 48 hours a week instead of 44.

Phyllis Bradley (b. 1925) worked in a tailoring factory at age fourteen:

We started at 8 in the morning. An hour for lunch. We would rush away home in a tram car. We'd only be home about quarter of an hour and then back, work till 6 o'clock at night. We would have a tea break mid-morning and mid-afternoon. We worked Saturday morning as well, 8 until 12.

It was common in 1940 to find men working 70-90 hours a week, often 6½ and 7 days. After France fell to the Germans in 1940, the Prime Minister broadcast to the nation: "the hours of labour are nothing compared with the struggle for life, honour, and freedom."

The fall of France in 1940 also prompted the cancellation of holidays. Holidays due then could be taken later, up to March 1941. In the spring of 1941 the Labour Co-ordinating Committee approved one week's paid holiday, with a public holiday on Whit Monday.

The summer of 1940 saw a great increase in the war effort. Factories were working twenty-four hours a day, seven days a week. A typical small factory making carburettors for fighter planes had workers on from 8.00 am to 7.00 pm every day. Some workers went on until midnight and then slept on sacks at the factory. Production rose at first but soon dropped back. People became just too tired.

A General Emergency Order (GEO) at the end of June 1940 for the engineering, shipbuilding, and metal industries tried to restrict working to a 60-hour week for women and young people (48 hours for those under sixteen). The GEO did not affect the long hours for men. Despite the laws, in 1941 a survey of 160 factories found some women and young people illegally working more than 60 hours a week.

In 1943 there was strong pressure to keep working hours down for young people, to 48 hours for those over sixteen and 44

30 Girls check the bands on Stirrup Hand Pumps — used to put out fires caused by incendiary bombs. By 1943, more than three quarters of British boys and more than two thirds of British girls aged fourteen to seventeen were working in some vital industry.

for those under sixteen. But the demands of war production made this difficult. It was agreed that where necessary, young people under sixteen could work up to 48 hours a week. Over sixteen, they could work up to 52 hours. 55 hours would be allowed for urgent work.

From 1944 on, the hours did reduce somewhat. Women were then working "only" 50-55 hours a week.

Women at work

40% of workers in the aircraft industry, and 52% of workers in chemicals and explosives were female — as were one third of workers in shipbuilding and heavy engineering. The railways too had over 100,000 females doing work that had been done by males before the war.

8 Family and Home Life

Home life changed with so many mothers working (making shells in munitions factories, driving lorries, welding, fighting fires . . .) and with so many fathers away in the forces. From mid-1941 the number of day nurseries for young children increased. By late 1942 over 65,000 children were in some 1,450 local authority nurseries. By 1944 some 70, 000 children were being minded by "daily guardians".

There were also, by mid-1941, 660 hostels in England and Wales and 230 residential nurseries for children orphaned by the Blitz and others in need of special care.

Births

There were actually 2 million *fewer* children under fourteen in 1939 than there had been in 1914. The birth rate in Britain was dropping from the 1870s until 1941 (when it was the lowest since recording began). In 1942 the rate suddenly went up, to the

31 A wartime home scene, with the absent sailor father's picture on the mantlepiece.

highest since 1931. This upward trend went on until 1947.

Of the 255,000 births between 1940 and 1945, about 40% (102,000) were illegitimate. Before the war as many as 30% of babies were conceived outside marriage — but in 70% of these cases the parents then married. In wartime, only 40% then married. Some of these illegitimate children were born to married women whose husbands were away in the forces. Some returning husbands simply accepted these children, but divorce did increase greatly.

Housing

Over 2 million houses had been damaged by mid-1941 (60% of these in London). By the end of the war, this figure was 3¾ million. ¼ million houses were beyond repair. In central London, only 10% of houses escaped damage.

As homes were damaged and destroyed, more and more families were living in unsatisfactory conditions. By the winter of 1942, over 100,000 families were in houses already condemned before the war. And 200,000 more families were in houses that would have been condemned in normal times. 2½ million more people were living in unrepaired houses.

Rest centres set up for the homeless were badly overcrowded and meant only for short stays. But many people remained in them for weeks because they had nowhere else to go. Some 200,000 went through these, about one in seven of London's homeless.

Some homeless children and their families squatted in empty flats and houses. Councils were sometimes able to requisition empty houses if the owners would not let them or live in them themselves.

Because of the shortage of barracks, some children shared their homes with army men billeted with the family.

Many people were forced to move several times during the war and, for the civilian population of about 38 million, there were some 60 million changes of address.

32 Essex. A boy shows his sister relics collected from a German plane which crashed nearby. The crack in the wall was caused by a bomb falling behind the house. There was a great shortage of builders and materials for house repairs.

33 "Save Fuel, Snap off Hitler's Nose" was a reminder to turn off lights.

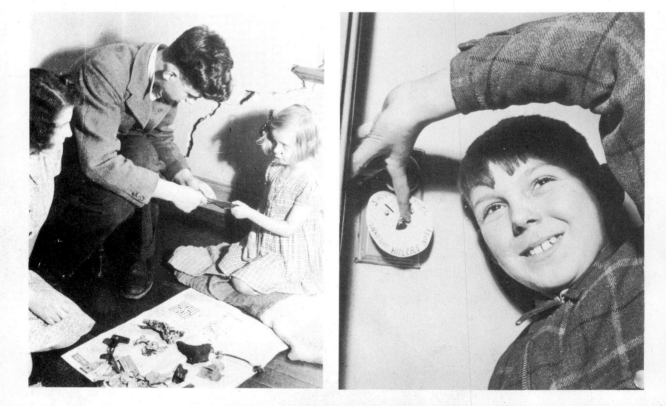

Household goods

Spending on household goods fell by nearly two thirds between 1938 and 1944. Households became increasingly shabby as replacement of household items was so difficult. New furniture was not on ration, but householders could only spend up to a fixed number of points and there were not always items to buy. Newly-weds found it very difficult to set-up home. Nearly 90% lived with in-laws. Colin Ward (b. 1924):

> The secondhand trade was booming. Commodities that were useless just before the war suddenly became valuable.

Some items (like new alarm clocks) were just unobtainable. And by 1944 95% of household spending was on price-controlled goods.

Bedding and household linen were hard to get — or very expensive. Extras such as tablecloths were generally turned into curtaining or made into clothes. Items like baby baths, fireguards, prams were all very short. Thick, plain white cups became standard. Cutlery was so short that some cafés chained spoons, to stop them being "liberated".

34 With little central heating, most families sat round a coal or gas fire for warmth. But coal was very short. By 1944-45 people were using 4 million tons less coal and anthracite in their grates than before the war.

Household hardware production was down some 60%. John Conder (b. 1935):

> By the end of the war we had to make special patches to fit in the holes of the saucepans we'd got left.

Children first saw "utility" furniture in 1942. It was very simple and limited in the material and designs that could be used. By 1943 only utility furniture was being made. There was only enough for the most urgent needs. Licences to buy the furniture were given first to people who had been bombed out or were setting up home for the first time. Many articles came under the utility scheme — including home electrical appliances and carpets.

Light and heat

Lighting in homes varied. There was a great expansion of electricity during the 1930s. Phyllis Bradley's (b. 1925) Glasgow home had had electricity since 1935: "It was wonderful. We used to be afraid of the gas light." But John Rodgers (b. 1929) living in London had only oil light: "We had no gas or electricity. We had oil lamps on the wall." For country cottages, electric light was still very much a luxury — as were piped water and indoor toilets.

There were local shortages of coal in the first two winters of the war. By 1941 this had become a much more widespread

problem. Children joined queues at the coal dumps. The notices said "coal . . . for those who can carry it away". The difficulty of transporting the coal was one reason for the shortages. The shortage of miners was more important. Children joined in the public campaign to save fuel. Baths were to be only 5 inches (12.5 centimetres) deep, fewer lights should be used, and so on.

> We could only have about a bag of coal a week. There was no fire after 7 o'clock at night. Once a day you could heat up water. We had the gas ring, it was in the fireplace at the side of the fire. So you could use the two rings and heat from the fire for your cooking and heating water. (Phyllis Bradley, b. 1925)

Large iron ranges (using coal) were the main way of cooking in country areas. Gas or electric cookers were increasingly common in towns and cities. In 1944 the Ministry of Fuel and Power urged households to cut down on gas and electricity. "Remember, gas and electricity are made from coal." Paraffin was also in short supply.

John Rodgers (b. 1929):

> For heat we used to get a bit of sand and cement and coal dust and mix it. And we used to burn it. It used to spit lumps of concrete. If a tree fell down we used to grab the wood quick as we could.

Washing

A home electric washing machine with a wringer on the top was available, but expensive. Many people used the steam wash-houses and public baths.

> They used to have old scrubbing boards. Big boilers. They'd heat them up with coal. Put your wet clothes through the wringer. It was really a hard job. The corporation had baths. We went there once a week. Soap was scarce. We took a piece of cloth, put oatmeal in, and cleaned ourselves with that. (Phyllis Bradley, b. 1925)

Religion

Thousands of churches were damaged and there were fewer clergy around. But religious broadcasting did increase. And Mass Observation surveys (Mass Observation began in the 1930s as a new social survey organization) found many people turning to prayer even if they did not attend any church. Children did not hear church bells. These were silenced at the beginning of the war — only to be used as warning of invasion.

35 1941, Liverpool. This docker did not get home until 9.30 at night, but his five-year-old daughter waited up. Parents were working extra-long hours. In the corner is the all-important radio. Listening-in greatly increased during the war.

9 Food and Drink

Rationing

Official food rationing did not start until 8 January 1940. The government was reluctant, but the public felt that rationing would be the fairest way of sharing out the goods which were already short. Some shop-keepers were already running their own unofficial ration scheme by refusing to sell out to people who could afford to buy a lot at once. "Under the counter" was the wartime phrase for scarce goods saved for favourite customers.

First to be rationed were butter, sugar, bacon and fat. In March, meat was added (rationed not by weight but by price). Tea was added in July. Cheese, cooking fat, sweets and other foods were added gradually.

By 1944 slightly over half of food spending was on rationed foods.

While Britain was not starving, rationing was a strain. Consumption of food did fall by one eighth between 1938 and 1944. John Conder (b. 1935):

> My mother collected the week's rations and put it in a little pile in the middle of the table. And then she started crying. I can't remember being hungry. But because of my age, by the end of the war I just hadn't ever tasted some things.

36   1942. London housewives queue to collect their food ration books from a mobile unit.

Ration books contained coupons that could be exchanged for various staple foods (for example, coupons for sugar, or coupons for meat). People registered with their normal grocer. The amounts allowed varied during the war. The buff general ration book was for adults and children over six. The green child's book was for the under-sixes. Young children were allowed only half the adult amount of meat. Nearly everyone over six had the same ration. But there were some exceptions, such as farm workers and miners, who were allowed extra cheese.

> Instead of having stewed meat we'd have stew with lumps of bread in it. (John Conder, b. 1935)

> Our meat was mutton. Three penny-worth of mutton. That was our Sunday food and however long it lasted during the week. That's the only meat I can ever remember. And an old rabbit now and again. (John Rodgers, b. 1929)

37 1941. Chocolate and ice cream had become scarce — but carrots were plentiful. Adrian Walker (b. 1938) was about seven when he had his first ice cream: "It was pink and made me sick. My stomach wasn't used to it. One had been on a very plain diet."

Christmas meant some extra food rations. For example, in 1944 children from six months to eighteen years old were allowed an extra ½ lb (225 grammes) of sweets during December. Extra sugar, margarine, and dates were also allowed. There were more turkeys and Christmas puddings than the year before.

By 1941 adverts were asking please keep milk chocolate for the children, as supplies were low. John Rodgers (b. 1929):

> We used to go to the sweet shop, ask 'em if they had any old cardboard boxes. We used to see if any sweet were stuck underneath, in the bottom. And then we used the cardboard to keep the fire going.

Restaurants

Restaurant meals were not rationed. Factory canteens and non-profit British Restaurants were set up. By 1944 people were eating some 170 million meals out, compared to 79 million in 1941. Restaurant owners received a rationed amount of food based on the number of meals they regularly served. Meals were limited to one main course and a top charge of five shillings (25p). This top charge was ignored for "better" restaurants.

Controlling food supplies

By 1943 there was no white bread in Britain, no ice-cream, no bananas, no lemons. People were also on small rations of the following: meat, milk, eggs, butter, margarine, cooking fats, bacon, ham, sugar, tea, preserves, sweets and chocolate.

There were other ways of controlling the consumption of food — such as taxation,

38 A small boy shopping for sweets has coupons ▶ cut out from his ration book by the shop assistant. In July 1942 the last extension of rationing meant each person could buy up to 8 oz (225 grammes) of chocolate and sweets a month, raised to 12 oz (340 grammes) in October. Sweet rationing went on until 1953. (1954 was the end of all rationing.)

39 1941. Nettle puree on potato slices. Country herb committees advised on which common weeds or wild plants could be used. The Ministry of Food tried to encourage the use of unusual food, but busy housewives mostly just reduced the servings of ordinary food.

dilution, price-fixing and substitution. A "points" system further restricted buying of canned meat, canned fish, canned beans, dried fruit, rice, sago, tapioca, dried pulses, canned fruit, canned peas, canned tomatoes, canned milk, breakfast cereals, oat flakes, syrup, treacle and biscuits. Different foods were worth different numbers of points. In 1942 each person had 20 points per week to spend as they chose. Bread (until after the war), potatoes, green vegetables, fruit and fish were sold on a first-come-first-served basis.

By 1942 victories by the Japanese in the Far East had affected Britain's supplies of rice, sugar and tea (as well as raw materials like rubber and tin).

Some extra food was available to pregnant women and children under five — especially eggs. Real eggs were in short supply. Pregnant and nursing mothers, children and invalids were also guaranteed a certain amount of milk. The general public was rationed to what was left.

A National Milk Scheme was started in 1940. Before the war only about half the school population were receiving one third of a pint (186 ml) of milk free each day. By the end of the war, nearly three quarters were. Milk production as a whole fell during the war years, but much less milk was being used in manufactured foods.

By 1943 nearly a third more milk was being drunk, and about a third more vegetables were being eaten than before the war. One fifth less meat was being eaten, two fifths less poultry and fish, nearly a third less sugar and syrups, only about half as much citrus and other fruits, and nearly one fifth less oils and fats. The nutritional value of the diet available was as good or better than in 1939 — though the food was less varied.

A 1941 *Daily Express* headline described "Oranges today are a 5 to 2 chance". A shipload arrived, but the paper warned that the supply would not go far. A sign on one fruit stand said: "Oranges For The Children". Bananas were even rarer than oranges. Adrian Walker (b. 1938):

> I was seven the first time I saw a banana. I remember the name of the kid that had it.

There were efforts to re-create favourite flavours and tastes that were hard-to-get. Phyllis Bradley (b. 1925, in Scotland):

> We used to boil up turnips, let them go cold and mix in some sugar. That gave you the flavour of bananas. Everyone was doing it.

For the very richest children, there was always a small Black Market of luxury foods such as grapes and melons at very high prices.

Canteens

Food in school and factory canteens was good and cheap. Very poor children actually ate better during the war than before. Many more children were receiving free or subsidized school meals. In 1940 about one thousand adults and children a day were being fed free in a canteen in London's bombed dockland area. There was no gas or water in the houses, so that no cooking could be done. Cafés and coffee shops had all closed.

By May of 1941 there were some 170 "Londoners' Meal Service Centres", mostly in school buildings. There were also over 190 mobile canteens and 27 community kitchens set up by voluntary organizations. Feeding in rest centres and shelters had become better. Canteen trains were running in the Underground.

Wartime food

Manufactured foods were much less varied: for instance, children had many fewer kinds of biscuits. Between 1942 and 1944 numbers rather than brand names were used on soft drinks. But some children's favourites were freely available in the Second World War. "Goody, goody they're not rationing Ovaltine Rusks," beamed the small child in one advert.

National Wholemeal bread was not so well liked. Until mid-1942 it was possible to buy white bread, even though some flour mills had been damaged. Only about 5% of bread bought was the National Wholemeal loaf. From March 1942 shipping problems meant that all bread was brown. Only about 14% of people preferred Wholemeal, even though it was better for health.

From 1942 dried foods were imported from the USA. Dried eggs, milk, potatoes, and cabbage could all be bought for home use. Dried meat went to restaurants and canteens. Dried egg was very popular.

Adrian Walker (b. 1938) remembers:

We used to get food parcels from a friend in South Africa. Lots of families did.

Farming

Before the war, some two thirds of Britain's food was imported. By the end, the proportion was less than one third. The increase in home production was made possible by adding 6 million more acres to the 12 million that were being ploughed before 1939.

Farmers worked every day and at night as well, concentrating on grain and vegetables. The decline in livestock and poultry caused milk production to fall by 4% and egg production by one half. There was only one third of the amount of pig meat, only four fifths the lamb and mutton, and five sixths the beef and veal.

By March 1940 many young agricultural workers had been lost to the services or industry. There was a great shortage of labour. The "Land Army" brought in thousands of girls and women to help on the farms. At harvest times older school-children and city workers also came to help. Many stayed in farm holiday camps for long weekends or a fortnight at a time. They paid a low fee for board and lodging — and the farmer paid them for their help. By 1943 there were over one thousand harvest camps housing some 63,000 town children during the summer holidays. Evacuees too helped with farm production.

40 1940. Boys collected swill to be fed to pigs. There were thousands of "Pig Clubs" that supported animals fed on kitchen waste.

John Conder (b. 1935):

My father came from London one time to help. It was a long day's work. I spent most of my time chasing rabbits. My brother was seven years older so he worked properly.

By 1943 there were also nearly 40,000 Italian prisoners of war helping in the fields. British soldiers and American GIs helped too.

In addition, more food was produced by city homes, as John Rodgers (b. 1929 in London) remembers:

We used to have to grow our own food in the garden. You grew all your veg, had a couple of chickens, couple of rabbits.

War against waste
A 1940 bulletin from the Ministry of Food urged everyone to drink three cups of tea a day instead of four, to save on shipping space for war material.

Harriet Ward (b. 1930):

At boarding school at the end of the war there was constant nagging. You weren't supposed to leave anything on your plate. There was this phrase "think of the starving children of Europe".

Children like John Rodgers (b. 1929) were anyway not wasters:

We used to have to scrounge really, get stale bread, pennyworth of specks (that was specky apples, any kind of fruit).

41 1941. Evacuees staying in the country set off to help on allotments. "Dig for Victory" was the slogan. The number of allotments nearly doubled from 1939 to 1943. John Rodgers (b. 1929): "We used to go round the streets with a bucket, picking up horse manure for the allotment."

10 Clothing

Babies and young children

By the late 1930s babywear was much simpler than before. Looser, softer materials were becoming more common. Babies were still wearing flannel or flannelette petticoats. Daygowns and nightgowns had long sleeves with lace at the wrists and neck. The "baby bag" began in the 1930s, with a buttoned flap at the bottom.

Matching dress and baggy knicker sets for girls were very popular up to about age twelve. Puff sleeves and Peter Pan collars were worn up to mid-teens. Small boys were often dressed in "buster suits" — with square-cut pant leg to mid-thigh. "Breechette" sets were popular outerwear for both boys and girls up to about five years. These had a matching hat or cap, coat, and leg coverings which were full round the seat, then tapered down the leg. Zips or buttons fastened these. There were straps under the instep of the foot.

School uniforms

Public and private schools were very demanding about school uniforms, but things were less strict in state elementary schools. Many state schools did try to have at least some identifying mark, however, such as a school badge for hats, caps and jackets. Schoolgirls might wear a navy serge gymslip with three box pleats back and front, navy knickers, white blouse, school tie, blazer, hat, double-breasted navy nap coat, black or brown stockings (held up by suspenders or garters), and black or brown lace-up shoes. Most boys, too, were soberly dressed in grey suit, shirt, tie, three-quarter hose, black or brown shoes, cap and blazer.

Out-of-school

Children's coats in the 1930s were well-known for their fitted style, often with velvet or velveteen trimming, and much top-stitching.

Sandals and plimsolls were popular out-of-school wear. By the end of the thirties the new idea of children's play clothes for seaside and country began.

42 1940. "Dickie suits" were popular for toddlers.

New war items

As the war started, children's clothes were still being produced much as before. There were some interesting new items. Some red velvet party cloaks had bright white linings, so that they could be worn reversed when going home in the blackout.

"Siren suits" were devised as simple, one-piece children's coveralls with hoods, that could be quickly put on for going to the shelter. There were large pockets for torch, identification card, etc. (Everyone had a personal identification card.) The suits also had a shoulder tab for holding the strap of a gas mask.

Hand embroidery and smocking on girls' dresses was still plentiful at the start of the war. Appliqué, piping, pin-tucking, and top-stitching was also widely used on children's clothes. When *Pinocchio*, Disney's second full-length colour cartoon arrived in Britain in 1940, characters from the film appeared on bibs and many other clothes.

Rationing and shortages

Clothes rationing began in June 1941. Most people welcomed this as the fairest way of sharing what goods were available. Unlike with food, customers were not registered with any one particular clothes shop. Some groups, including older children, had extra coupons.

Wartime rationing and shortages encouraged parents to buy their children the best-quality clothes they could. The same number of coupons had to be given up for a cheap dress as for a well-made one that could give years of wear.

Shortages of children's clothing became a very big problem during the war. Baby-wear and children's shoes were especially scarce. Adult clothing was much less difficult, partly because so many adults went into the forces. A *Daily Express* article in 1944 reported that stocks of children's clothes were more than a fifth lower than in 1943. Some stocks were destroyed by flying-bombs, but more important was the shortage of labour in clothing factories. Already more than a quarter of workers were girls under sixteen. Clothes rationing did release thousands of workers for the war factories.

Poor children

Many children were, anyway, very short of clothing when the war began. The evacuation of city children brought attention to the fact that many were especially in need of footwear, underwear, and nightwear. An inspection of some 25,000 Newcastle-upon-Tyne evacuees showed that about 13% of the children had "insufficient footwear", 9% had "insufficient day clothing", and 12% had "insufficient underwear or nightwear". Teachers thought that some other children were not being sent for evacuation because their parents were unable to afford clothing for them. In areas of high unemployment such as Wales and Scotland some children were still barefoot. Colin Ward (b. 1924):

> In 1943 I was accosted by little barefoot boys on the street in Glasgow begging "Gi's a penny mister" or "soljar".

Saving on clothing

"Utility" clothing was started in 1941, made of specified cloths. The result was a rise in standards, and prices were closely controlled. Children's utility coats were about 40% cheaper than similar non-utility coats. All sorts of regulations affecting clothes for children followed, cutting out much of the extra styling and trimming. Some changes became permanent: for example, after 1942 matching frock and

43 Young people up to age eighteen were mostly clothed from the juvenile departments. Teenage girls (called "maids") moved from wearing the Liberty bodice as underwear to small-size women's corselettes. Few clothes were produced specially for them. Even their dresses were mainly large sizes of styles worn by their little sisters.

knicker sets were not made again. The many rows of fine top-stitching on children's coats were limited, and stayed much reduced after the war. The 1941 Order did not allow boys taking less than Leeds size six (about eleven years old) to have long trousers. Trousers for older boys were not allowed to have turn-ups.

"Make-do-and-mend" was the rule for children's as well as adults' clothing. By 1943 the amount of clothes available for British citizens was about half what it was pre-war. Spending on clothing fell by over one third between 1938 and 1944. Mothers were encouraged to use up every bit of old clothes in clothing the family. A *Daily Mirror* article in 1942 passed on tips of how others were managing. One mother had used a man's coat to make an overcoat and pair of trousers for a seven-year-old boy. But a mother of eight pointed out that this cutting down and remaking had always been necessary with large, poor families.

John Conder (b. 1935):

We made a lot of things out of barrage balloon stuff. Things were made out of old flying suits, parachutes.

Phyllis Bradley (b. 1925):

We would get blackout material (it wasn't rationed — the material we used

for the curtains) and we made up skirts. It's amazing how you managed to look smart. At least, we thought we did. And we'd have our coats dyed once they got sort of shabby-looking. Or perhaps shorten it, make a jacket.

John Rodgers (b. 1929):

We used to put cardboard in our shoes over the holes. And we used to make shoes. Have a piece of wood near enough the shape of your foot. Put pieces of leather straps or whatever you could find, nail 'em over.

Colin Ward (b. 1924):

Service in the army brought people in touch with a better standard of clothing. For many people, army boots were the best pair of boots they'd ever had.

Women and girls met the stocking shortage by using leg make-up. Phyllis Bradley (b. 1925):

We painted our legs. At first we put the line up the back to look like a seam, but it took too much time. It was a sort of can in a bottle. You'd have a thick pair of really serviceable stockings for work. But in the evening when we were going out we'd start with the leg make-up.

(Phyllis Bradley also remembers how headscarves and turbans became more widespread for women and girls, as did wearing trousers:

We had these aluminium curlers. Being in a factory, if we were going out in an evening we'd pin our hair up and put a turban on, just go to work like that. If you did go to the hairdresser, they didn't have all the styling they have now. You just got a perm.)

49

44 Utility sleeping suit for a four-year-old cost 18/9 (93p) and four clothing coupons. Utility clothes became about 80% of all clothes production.
▼

◄45 A WVS (Women's Voluntary Service) worker at a clothing exchange helps find clothes for a girl who lost all of hers when her home was destroyed the night before. (This jumper, and many other clothes, had been sent from America.)

"Clothing Exchanges" were backed by local councils and staffed mainly by the Women's Voluntary Service (WVS). These exchanges were a great help in trying to meet the needs of growing children. Old clothes could be handed in and were "priced" at a certain number of points. Some other article, worth similar points, could be taken in exchange. Similarly, public and private schools made appeals to "old boys" and "old girls" to turn in their old uniforms for re-use.

Harriet Ward (b. 1930):

At the age of twelve I madly wanted to join the Girl Guides — mainly to wear the uniform. Because of the war you couldn't get new uniforms, so I lost interest.

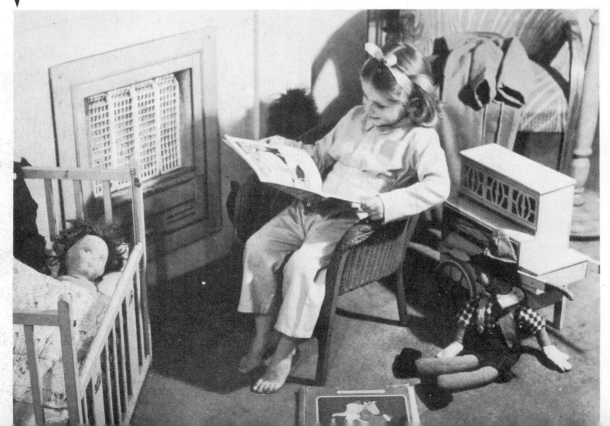

11 Health

Britain actually became healthier in the first few months of war, according to the *Daily Express*, November 1939. There were fewer cases of scarlet fever and diphtheria than in the same months of 1938. Deaths from scarlet fever, diphtheria, measles and influenza were down. Some 1½ million women and children had left the city streets for the fresh air of the country. Because of the blackout, children (and some adults as well) were going to bed earlier and getting more sleep.

Between 1939 and 1945 infant deaths per thousand live births went down from 51 to 46 in England and Wales, and from 69 to 56 in Scotland. Deaths from diphtheria showed a marked decrease, mainly because so many children were vaccinated free of charge. And while the rate of tuberculosis had risen greatly at the beginning of the war, this too was declining later on.

On the other hand, poor city children were still commonly found to have vermin, fleas, headlice, impetigo, and scabies. One third to one half of families in most cities were without baths or inside taps, so that keeping clean was difficult. And certainly industrial towns were still less healthy places for children than the country. The death rate of infants and children was higher in manufacturing areas.

Vitamin Welfare Scheme

A Vitamin Welfare Scheme for children began in late 1941. Blackcurrant juice (rich in vitamin C) and cod-liver oil (rich in vitamins A and D) were at first issued free for children under two. The juice later became orange and a small charge was made.

Hospitals and doctors

During the Second World War there was no National Health Service like that in Britain today. There were two kinds of hospitals. About a thousand voluntary hospitals were not publicly controlled at all. The local authority hospitals were overcrowded and bare, with very poor facilities.

The practice of a general doctor was in three parts. Doctors received a fee from the government for attending workers insured under the National Insurance scheme — but in 1938-39 no more than half the population was in fact covered by this. They received payment from the *families* of insured workers

46   1940. Blackout screens over hospital windows were sometimes decorated.

who consulted them. And they also took fees from wealthy patients.

By the end of the war there were many fewer doctors and dentists. Over a third had been called into the forces. About 10% of those who remained were over seventy. The call-up of doctors and bombings of hospitals made it that much harder for sick children to have the attention they needed.

The Government Emergency Scheme meant that voluntary hospitals had to keep some beds empty, waiting for possible victims of bombings. And so waiting lists for other treatment grew even longer.

The Beveridge Report

The *Beveridge Report* came out in December 1942, and 90% of the population favoured its ideas. Its plan was for a single overall scheme of social insurance — to include a new National Health Service and family allowances for children. The White Paper on "A National Health Service" appeared in 1944. The Service, to be set up after the war, was to be financed by taxation and would cover dentists and opticians, doctors and surgeons. All hospital treatment was to be free.

47   1944. Infants were taught basic first-aid.

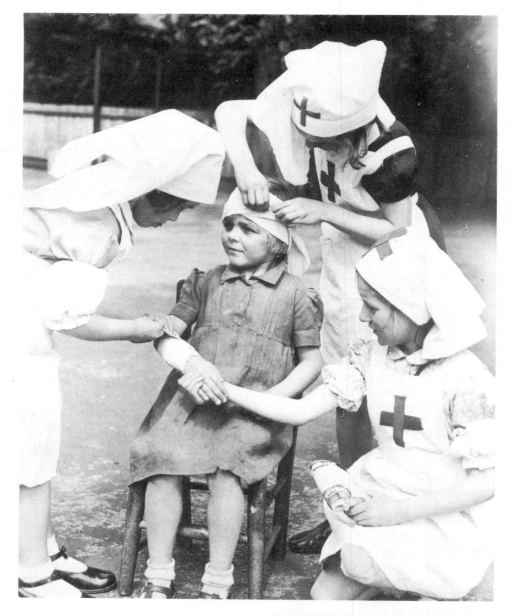

12 Transport

Railways

Reduced transport and the blackout were the two things people found most inconvenient during the war, according to Mass Observation. By 1943 fifty passenger trains had been lost in air raids and over 100,000 railway men had been called-up. Many passenger trains were taken over for troops. On the trains which were left, children rode with servicemen and women travelling home on leave, and war workers who were being sent miles from home on "Essential Jobs".

While total railway services were cut by

48 This government photo was meant to warn drivers to watch out for children. Because of the blackout, car headlights were all masked. Light shone only through narrow slits. Though there were fewer cars on the road, these killed more children than in peacetime. Front and rear bumpers were painted white to try to help visibility.

more than a third during the war, the need had greatly increased. By the winter of 1942-43 there were 10% fewer carriages — but goods traffic was up 50% and passenger travel up about 70%. Harriet Ward (b. 1930):

> All the corridors were full of people standing. Every train was choc-a-bloc. You were very lucky if you had a seat.

"Is Your Journey Really Necessary?" asked a famous wartime poster.
Colin Ward (b. 1924):

> Long distance train journeys were awful because the trains themselves were blacked out. Over the dim blue bulbs were pierced tin cans to reduce the light.

There was little if any food available on trains. By 1943 only 10% of dining cars were in use. Overcrowded buffets at stations displayed "sorry no . . . . " signs amid the cracked china.

Motor buses, trams and trolleybuses
Motor bus services (suffering from not enough staff and shortages of rubber tyres, petrol and spare parts) were being cut. In many places buses stopped by 9 o'clock at night (10 o'clock in larger cities). Children on London buses found bare wooden slatted seats. Because London lost so many buses in the bombings, outside buses from the provinces (in all sorts of colours) were seen in London streets. In September 1942 long-distance buses went off the roads and restrictions on railway travel were added.

Trams were being phased out over the 1930s — to be replaced largely by trolley-buses. These were not on a track but (like trams) drew on electric power through overhead wires. Trolleybuses often had their lines cut during the war by bombings.

On all public transport women had largely replaced male bus conductors, train guards, ticket collectors, and porters.

54

Motor cars
Few people could ride in private cars. Petrol rationing started a few weeks into the war, and after March 1942 the private motorist could only get petrol if essential for health or work. By late 1942, most private cars were simply being stored.

Signposts
In May 1940 the Minister of Transport announced that signposts helpful to an invading enemy were to be removed. Large signs on stations, main road signs, and so on, were therefore taken down — making travelling confusing for the British too! Railway stations within twenty miles of the east and south coasts were not labelled at all.

49   1940. Children act out a familiar scene. Hitch-hiking was very respectable during the war. In 1939 there were over 2 million cars and over 400,000 motorcycles in private use in Britain. By 1943 just 718,000 private cars and 124,000 motorcycles were being used, because of the shortage of petrol. Spending on petrol for private use was only 6% of what it was pre-war.

13 Holidays, Sports and Entertainments

Holidays by the seaside were difficult. The *Sunday Pictorial* of 25 July 1943 showed a picture of the crowd (including many children) at Waterloo Station trying to get a train to the coast. "Thousands waited for hours in vain. The rest travelled in agony." All these people were ignoring the Ministry of Transport's plea: Don't travel unless necessary. There were similar scenes at stations in big industrial towns all over Britain. John Rodgers (b. 1929):

> I didn't see the seaside till I was sixteen years old. And that was just Windsor.

"Holidays-at-Home"

"Holidays-at-Home" were promoted to keep people from travelling. Local amusements were organized. Children whose families could not have afforded to take them away on holiday anyway thus had the benefit of these extra attractions. There were some holiday camps for war workers — just communal wooden huts, but very popular.

ENSA and CEMA

Official recreation and entertainment was on a massive scale, in an effort to keep up morale. Young people working in factories saw ENSA concerts in the canteen. ENSA was the Entertainments National Service Association which organized all sorts of entertainments for the forces, and for civilians as well. Children in remote places had the chance to see performances by major London companies who, bombed out, went on tours of the provinces. CEMA, the Council for Education in Music and the Arts helped in this as well.

Christmas and birthdays

Christmas was hard to enjoy to the full. Phyllis Bradley (b. 1925):

> We didn't make much of Christmas at all between '39 and '43. People were working Christmas Day. Everyone wasn't at home.

The shortages, including the growing shortage of paper, made buying presents difficult — and wrapping them harder still.

50   A south coast resort, 1944. The boy uses an old flower-pot to make his castles. Production of children's buckets and spades (and many other non-essential items) was stopped in 1942.

From 1941 shopkeepers were not allowed to provide paper for wrapping or packing goods.

Birthdays too were rather low-key. Even when Princess Elizabeth celebrated her fifteenth birthday in 1941, the *Sunday Times* reported that the only party was having a few girl friends to tea, followed by a film show (including a few short reels taken by the Princess herself).

Sports

Sports were also played much less during the war. Not only were both professional and amateur sportsmen away in the forces, but sports grounds were being used for all sorts of other purposes — such as Home Guard drilling, growing food, and as prisoner of war camps. Spectator crowds were only one eighth to one quarter of pre-war numbers. Many people were working on Saturdays anyway. And air raids sometimes stopped play. By 1943 attendance at what football and cricket there was began to increase. The players were all teenagers, or men playing part-time from their main jobs in the forces and industry.

Cinema and theatre

Cinema and theatre attendance boomed during the war. Money spent on such entertainment more than doubled in the years 1938-44. The Wartime Social Survey found that 80% of fourteen to seventeen year olds went at least once a week to the cinema. 40% went at least twice a week.

Just before the war, in 1938, the first full-length cartoon film, Disney's *Snow White and the Seven Dwarfs*, was shown. *The Wizard of Oz* came out in 1939, *Gone With the Wind* in 1942, and *Dumbo* was first shown in Britain in 1941. There were also lots of war films. Phyllis Bradley (b. 1925):

> It was nicer to go to a love film or a comedy, something that took your mind away from the war.

Adrian Walker (b. 1938):

> At the Saturday morning pictures you had a singsong where you followed the bouncing ball. The words flashed on the screen and the ball bounced from word to word. This was before the film. You always had a cartoon. Then we had a Flash Gordon serial. Then the main film, which was always a cowboy film.

Children saw documentaries as well. Children in one Welsh village actually helped make one, called *The Silent Village*, in memory of the massacre in a Czech village called Lidice.

Newsreels too reminded children of what was happening in the war:

> The newsreels were unbelievable. You couldn't imagine it was really all happening. (Phyllis Bradley, b. 1925)

> At the very end of the war when the armies in Europe were opening the concentration camps, the newsreels were full of these horrific news items. There were these piles of corpses and walking skeletons. This was in a cinema full of children. I don't think it was wrong for us to see it. (Harriet Ward, b. 1930).

Unfortunately, the war came very close for some children. One Saturday afternoon in 1940 three hundred women and children were in a Brighton cinema watching a film called *It Could Happen to You*. A German bomber dropped two high-explosive bombs

51 1940. Worried faces at a children's matinee western. Adrian Walker (b. 1938): "People used to shout out to the hero that the villain was sneaking up behind." About one third of adults and four fifths of adolescents went to the pictures once a week or more. Phyllis Bradley (b. 1925): "We didn't have the large screens like today, it was much smaller."

through the cinema roof.

Many cinemas (including sixty in London) were destroyed by bombs. Places of public entertainment did close at times during the war, and during the Blitz attendances fell at first. But they soon recovered and the popularity of the cinema remained high. Part of the reason was that there was not much else to spend your money on. And some cinemas even offered shelter and entertainment for the whole night.

Ballrooms

Ballrooms were popular with older teenagers, like Phyllis Bradley (b. 1925):

We used to go to dancing class in an old church hall. In a year's time or less we were able to go to the ballroom. That was at the young age of seventeen. We went with our girlfriends. Your mother always said, now, remember, stay together, don't separate. We had quite a number of ballrooms in Glasgow. The first dance you would learn was a waltz, and then the quick-step, slow fox-trot, and then the tango. Once you had learned the tango you were really a dancer. It was a wonderful relaxation. You met such a variety. The forces were always coming and going. We used to put flowers in our hair. There were parties too, if anyone was going away abroad, or due to come home. There was very little in the way of drink. Just soft drinks in the ballrooms.

Radio and television

The radio was very important for entertainment as well as for news.

I used to love the *Children's Hour*. (John Conder, b. 1935)

There was *Monday Night at Eight* and

ITMA, which we listened to without fail. It was the highlight of the week. (Harriet Ward, b. 1930)

ITMA stood for "It's That Man Again". All the catch phrases caught on. There was a char lady called Mrs Mopp who used to say "Can I do you now, sir?" (Adrian Walker, b. 1938)

(A small boy trapped under a pile of rubble after a raid on Bath reportedly called out to the rescuers: "Can you do me now, sir?")

The newly begun television service closed down two days before the war began — but radio kept going and increased its staff, transmitters, and hours of broadcasting. Children listening to the nine o'clock news one night heard a loud boom as a bomb hit the side of the station — but the announcer paused only for a moment before finishing.

The request programme *Forces Favourites* was a link for scattered families. Servicemen and women could send a brief message with their record request.

Teenagers in factories listened to programmes as well:

That was a wonderful thing when they brought the radio in. We had *Music While You Work*. (Phyllis Bradley, b. 1925)

"Lord Haw-Haw" was William Joyce, an English traitor who broadcast from Germany for the Germans, in an effort to weaken British morale. Nearly a third of Britain listened to him regularly, for amusement. But his remarks could have their effects. John Conder (b. 1935):

Lord Haw-Haw said a boat my uncle was on had been destroyed — when it hadn't. This caused some disturbance in my family.

The *Brains Trust* was another popular programme.

Wireless sets

Crystal sets were the earliest way of listening to the wireless. But large valve sets with built-in speakers were part of the furniture in many homes by the late 1930s. John Rodgers (b. 1929):

We had a crystal set. You had ear-phones on and cat's whiskers. Tickle it till you got the sound.

Gramophones were still big and awkward, though without the original old trumpet. Wireless sets were sometimes combined with turntables to form the radiogram.

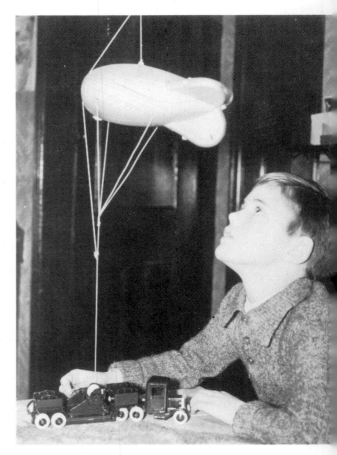

52 1939. Military toys were popular. The toy barrage balloon came complete with lorry-carrying winch. The real balloons floated over British cities which were likely to be an enemy target. Their purpose was to deter low-level enemy aircraft.

14 Toys and Games

We used to play air-raid shelters. Dig a hole in the ground and put four sticks up. A piece of roof across it. On top of that the earth and rubble. We'd sit in this little hole and bang away until the whole lot caved in on us. Then we had to free ourselves and crawl out. You used to have dirt in your hair.

John Conder (b. 1935) and other children of the forties acted out much of the real life they saw around them.

A playground ditty popular with children was:

Whistle while you work,
Old Hitler is a twerp,
He's half barmy
So's his army,
Whistle while you work.

It was also common to see the "V" for Victory sign chalked on playground walls. War games included pretending to be British Spitfire planes shooting down German Messerschmitts. In playground corners children swapped their treasured finds — bits of shrapnel, army buttons, cartridge cases.

Toys

Gradually, new toys became less and less available. There was only a very limited range. Local shops had only simple cheap toys — like a small plaster doll which you coloured yourself. In 1942 the growing shortage of materials meant that it was no longer allowed to make any toys using rubber, cork, hemp, kapok, celluloid, or certain plastics. Old, pre-war toys were therefore mended again and again. These included those of the 1920s when there had been a trend for plain, solid toys from which children could learn basic skills, and those of the 1930s, when synthetic materials like plastic had first been used.

In 1933, model cars and other vehicles had come out as accessories for the Hornby

53 1943. Children made what fun they could, as always. One of the War Emergency Information and Instructions (largely ignored) was "Do not allow your children to run about the streets".

model railway and between then and the war a large variety of these "Dinky toys" had come on to the market. Children in the 1940s cherished these old toys, and then after the war the Dinky range was widened still further.

Other pre-war games carried on. Harriet Ward (b. 1930):

We had things like Ludo and Snakes and Ladders. In our family we played Mah Jong.

Because toys were so hard to buy, much was homemade. Children made all sorts of things for themselves, out of scrap. An old bike part was the start of one bicycle, with a wooden handle for steering and old pram wheels added. (There were only about a third as many new bicycles available during wartime.)

54   A class of teenage girls practise their dancing.

Adrian Walker (b. 1938):

My Dad made us little vans one Christmas out of cardboard and filled them with sweets. Another Christmas he got hold of some moulds and some lead and made lots of soldiers. He and my mum painted them.

John Conder (b. 1935) helped make such soldiers himself:

We had a family business of melting the lead on the fire, ladle it into the moulds. One of us would trim and one would paint. We'd sell them at local stalls.

But for some children there was not much time for toys and games anyway . . . . John Rodgers (b. 1929):

I think that we were grown-up. Digging the garden, that was your fun.

15 Books and Newspapers

A *Snow White Magic Mirror Book* produced by the famous Dean's Rag Book Company was very popular in 1939 and '40. Children looking through the magic spectacles saw the pictures in 3-D. The new edition of *Rupert's Adventure Book* was published by the *Daily Express* in 1940, printed for the first time in full colour. The demand for books and newspapers increased during the war. This was partly because people wanted information on what was going on, partly because they had more time indoors, with the blacked-out evenings, and partly because they were looking for relief from the realities of war.

The cheap paperback book had only begun in the 1930s, with Penguin's first books appearing in 1935. But by 1943 the amount of paper available in Britain was only one fifth of pre-war supplies. Books, newspapers, comics, magazines all suffered. There was more use of libraries — but over 400 libraries were bombed out.

By 1943 papers that had been sixteen to twenty-four pages had been cut down to as few as six or four pages. Others just printed fewer copies. Staffs too were smaller. Teenage boys as well as older men kept the printing presses going.

In 1942, with the help of a press salvaged from their bombed school, some evacuated boys at Southborough produced their own magazine. Called *London and Local*, it included items by the boys themselves.

The newspapers left did not give much information on some things. There were no current weather reports, as these could have helped enemy bombers. Bombed places in Britain were not described by name. Many important developments in the war just could not be included.

Despite the censorship, the papers did tell children a lot of unpleasant things. John Rodgers (b. 1929):

> You read all about what was happening. You got hardened to it.

And children saw lots of advertisements for things which were hard or impossible to get. "Not till after the war," some adverts said. Manufacturers wanted their products remembered.

55 Four Liverpool boys share a single comic, 1941. The growing shortage of paper meant that many children's comics simply were not published.

16 Mischief and Crime

The crime rate was generally lower during the war. ("Offences against Defence Regulations" covered such matters as showing light during the blackout.) But *children* stealing and otherwise in trouble *was* a growing problem. The Chairman of a London Juvenile Court pointed out (*Sunday Pictorial*, 1942) that the number of boys and girls in trouble with the police had increased by nearly a third since the start of the war.

> . . . the breaking up of families by evacuation; fathers away on active service, mothers at work all day in munition factories, irregular schooling, the closing of many clubs and evening institutes; the black-out; the night life of the public air raid shelters; streets of bombed houses with all their possibilities for adventure . . . .

> We have before us in the courts boys and girls of fifteen and more who can barely read. They are mostly children who trickled back after a month or two in the evacuation areas to find their old schools bombed or closed. They were allowed to roam the neighbourhood in little gangs, to explore the ruins, to hang about the streets. Is it surprising that so many of them go wrong?

Parents were urged to see that children used their spare time well. Besides suggesting the Scouts or Guides, the Chairman also mentioned the Junior Service Corps.

56 1941. Hanging on behind. Children had more chance to get into mischief with all the disruptions at school and parents away and working long hours. The number of young people under seventeen found guilty of breaking the law in England and Wales rose by over one third between 1939 and 1941. Reported petty stealing rose by 200%.

17 The War Ends

"VE" Day

On 1 May 1945 German radio announced that Hitler was dead. By the evening of 7 May it was clear to the world that the war in Europe had ended. But the official announcement was not until 8 May, "Victory in Europe" Day. Everyone celebrated, and 9

57 1945. A VE Day celebration. Street parties took place all over the country.

May was a holiday too. In Glasgow:

> Everyone just went mad. We went to town to George Square, drinking lemonade, toasting. All the soldiers were being carried high, singing. That went on for days. (Phyllis Bradley, b. 1925)

In Taunton, Somerset:

> We had a big party at the end of the street. I collected wood for the bonfire. They had an effigy of Hitler which they burnt. (Adrian Walker, b. 1938)

In London red, white, and blue ribbons decorated the hair of young children. Eros in Piccadilly had been hidden by scaffolding and sandbags. Young people climbed all over the statue, cheering wildly. People danced in the streets. Bonfires were lit, fireworks let off. Lamps lit the public buildings. For many young children, this was their first night of peace. They heard Churchill tell the crowds "This is your victory . . . ". Many were outside Buckingham Palace cheering as the King, Queen, and the two young Princesses came out onto the balcony. But there was still sadness for the many who had lost family, for disabled ex-soldiers, and those without homes. (On VE night some 12,000 people still slept in the London Underground because they had nowhere else to go.)

"VJ" Day

The Japanese surrendered on 14 August, "VJ" Day. Atomic bombs dropped by the Americans on the Japanese cities of Hiroshima and Nagasaki speeded the end of the war in that area. Many fathers, uncles, or brothers of British children had died in Japanese prisoner of war camps. But for most people in Britain this part of the war had seemed far away.

General election

A general election was held in July. Clement Attlee became the Labour Prime Minister for the next six years. The mood of the country was for reforms. "Building a new and better world" was the slogan. In summer 1945 a new universal family allowance began, paid to the mother, for the second and all further children. The Welfare State began in 1948 with the new National Insurance scheme and National Health Service.

Shortages continue

But shortages continued long after the war ended. Adrian Walker (b. 1938) went off to scout camp in 1947.

> My father made me a kind of mattress and stuffed it with straw and grass. My mum made me a sleeping bag that was just two blankets sewn together. I was fantastically well-equipped compared to other kids.

58   1948. A seven-year-old drives the tractor while his father loads. The war prompted the introduction of more machines in farming because manpower was so short. There were only 56,000 tractors in 1939 — but over 200,000 by the end of the war. The number of farm horses dropped by over 100,000. Still, farmers of the 1940s lacked many of the aids on today's farms.

Foods, too, were still on ration for years. Harriet Ward (b. 1930) went to America in 1947 to University:

I managed to get a place on a converted troop ship. In the dining room at supper-time were white rolls. We were still tied up at the quayside. I thought, I'm still in England and I can have white bread and they're still eating brown. In America I felt incredibly guilty about the good living and the waste of food.

1945 was a time of world-wide bad harvests and droughts. The disorder of war added to the food crisis. In early 1946 the world wheat shortage meant a cut in bacon, poultry and eggs. By mid-1946 bread went on the ration (it had not been during the war), and this rationing went on until July 1948.

Because meat supplies were short, whale-meat was common in butcher's shops in 1947 — but never very popular. A tropical fish called snoek was also brought in. Despite government efforts to encourage eating such novel foods, they did not sell very well.

It was 1950 before milk rationing ended — and flour, eggs and soap were no longer controlled.

Fuel too continued to be a problem, especially in the very cold winter of 1947. John Conder (b. 1935):

I went to the railway yard, scraping the empty tracks. I had a girlfriend. I thought she'd like a bag of coal dust.

Clothing

With clothing too, things took a long while to get better. Price controls on children's clothes did not end until 1952. Four months after the war was over, the clothes ration was at its lowest yet. In August 1945 there were great queues as usual in children's departments. Supplies of infant shoes and socks were less than half what they were in 1943. Some children were being fitted out using "demob" coupons. These had been

59 A "Blitz-site experimental playground", 1948. The object was to keep children safely occupied, away from the dangerous bombed-out buildings on the streets.

given to their fathers as they were being demobbed, or released from the forces. The coupons could be used for any kind of civilian clothing. Some temporary changes in clothing caused by shortages in the war became permanent. One example was the switch to ankle socks for schoolgirls in the early 1940s because of the shortage of stockings.

An important development was the growth of shops and departments for teenage girls, who had been much neglected. Teenager Princess Margaret was one of the first to move to the famous "New Look" fashion of 1947. Younger children too saw changes in their clothes. For example, man-made fibres were being used more — including nylon for baby dresses and swimsuits. Infant boys were being put in trousers with bib-and-brace tops instead of the old breech-ettes.

Housing

In the summer of 1946 children in some homeless families found themselves squatting in Nissen huts in old army camps. By the end of August over 20,000 people had moved into the camps. Other squatters then took over empty flats and homes in central London but were soon moved out. (Some children were still in army camps five years later!)

Over 160,000 Prefab houses were finally produced. These were meant to be temporary but became permanent homes for many. Some children were living in homes built by their fathers. The self-build housing movement was started after the war in 1949 by ex-servicemen still desperate to house their families.

Television

On 9 June 1946 there was a great Victory Parade in London. A few children saw two hours of the parade on the newly resumed BBC television service (its second day). This was a celebration of better and brighter times — but they would take a while to come.

60 A family in overcrowded housing, 1949. The shortage was still desperate.

Date List

1933	Adolf Hitler rises to power in Germany
1936	George VI becomes King
1937	(May) Neville Chamberlain becomes Conservative PM
1938	(spring) Hitler takes over Austria
	(September) Chamberlain sees Hitler, lets him take German-speaking areas of Czechoslovakia
1939	(March) Hitler takes rest of Czechoslovakia
	Britain promises support to Poland against German attack
	(April) Military conscription announced in Britain
	(1 September) German troops move into Poland
	Official British government's evacuation starts
	New BBC television service closes down
	(3 September) Britain's ultimatum to Germany to leave Poland expires
	Chamberlain announces Britain at war with Germany
	BBC radio opens one "Home Service"
1940	(January) Food rationing begins
	(May) First deliberate bombing on mainland Britain
	Winston Churchill becomes PM of coalition government
	Local Defence Volunteers (later Home Guard) formed
	(May, June) Germans occupy Belgium and France
	Evacuation of British soldiers home to Britain from Dunkirk
	(June) Italy, led by Mussolini, joins German side
	(summer to 1945) Germans occupy Channel Islands
	(July) Collecting salvage made compulsory
	(August - October) "Battle of Britain"
	(August) First bombing of civilian Britain (London)
	(September-May '41) "The Blitz"
1941	(June) Clothes rationing begins
	(December) Japanese attack US Navy at Pearl Harbour, Hawaii — also attack Americans in Philippines and British possessions of Hong Kong, Malaya, Burma
	Britain declares war on Japan
	Germany and Italy declare war on US (Japan their ally)
	USA into war, supporting Britain and allies
1942	"Utility" clothes, furniture, etc. begin
	(December) Beveridge Report published, urging National Health Service
1944	Butler Education Act, secondary education required for all
	(6 June) D-Day landing of Allies in France

(12 June-mid-August) VI "flying-bombs" by Germans

(September-March '45) V2 rockets by Germans

1945 (4 May) German forces surrender

(8 May) VE Day, "Victory in Europe"

(14 August) VJ Day, "Victory over Japan"

(July) Clement Attlee becomes Labour PM

1946 (8 June) BBC television service resumes

1947 School-leaving age raised to fifteen

1948 (July) National Insurance Scheme and National Health Service start

1954 End of all rationing

Books for Further Reading

Non-Fiction

Calder, Angus, *The People's War*, Panther, 1971

Chamberlain, E.R., *Life in Wartime Britain*, Batsford, 1972

Fitzgibbon, Constantine, *The Blitz*, Corgi, 1974

Harrison, Tom, *Living Through the Blitz*, Collins, 1976

Longmate, Norman, *How We Lived Then*, Hutchinson, 1971

Autobiography

Gershon, Karen (editor), *We Came as Children*, Victor Gollancz, 1966 (collective auto-biography of refugee children, based on 234 contributors)

Hannam, Charles, *Almost an Englishman*, André Deutsch, 1979 (Hannam came as refugee in 1939, book describes war years in Britain)

Johnson, B.S. (editor), *The Evacuees*, Victor Gollancz, 1968 (collection of essay memories of some of the 4 million children evacuated at some time during the war)

Perry, Colin, *Boy in the Blitz*, Leo Cooper, 1973

Glossary

billet	temporary assigned place to live
Blitz	a word taken from the German "Blitzkrieg", meaning "lightning war"; heavy constant air raids
conscription	compulsory enrolment for military service
crystal set	simple wireless receiving set. A delicate wire, called a cat's whisker, was put in contact with a crystal to direct the current, so that the sound was heard
demob	de-mobilize, let out of military service
Dominions	countries outside Britain under sovereignty of British crown. In Statute of Westminster (1931) this includes Canada, Australia, New Zealand, South Africa, Irish Free State, Newfoundland
"enemy aliens"	Germans, Austrians, Czechs living in Britain (including refugees) during the war
evacuation	sending people out of areas likely to be bombed to areas considered safer
Fifth Column	spies, people living in Britain who might be helping the Germans
flying-bombs	V1 pilotless small planes sent by Germans; when they ran out of fuel, the engine cut and crashed to earth exploding; also called "buzz bombs" and "doodle bugs"
Hurricane	type of RAF single-seater fighter plane during the war (two thirds of total)
internment	confining people, for example in camps, in order to keep an eye on them. "Enemy aliens" were interned during the war
Nazis	members of German Nationalist Socialist Party, led by Hitler
pill-box defences	miniature forts put up beside highways and on street corners from which shots could be fired at enemy in case of invasion
ration	fixed share or allowance of what is available
refugee	someone leaving his/her country because of pressures there, taking refuge elsewhere
shrapnel	shell holding bullets; a time fuse bursts the shell and scatters the bullets in a shower
Spitfire	type of RAF single-seater fighter plane during the war (one third of total)
Sudetenland	German-speaking area of Czechoslovakia as of 1938
utility	made for usefulness, provided so that people can be supplied in spite of price rises
V2 rockets	faster, more destructive rockets than V1 flying-bombs; also pilotless; could not be heard before they exploded

The author warmly thanks the following for contributing personal memories to this book:

Phyllis Bradley ➤
(b.1925)

1943

John Conder
(b.1935)

Charles Hannam
(b.1926)

Henry Ricketts
(b.1923)

John Rodgers
(b.1929)

Kathleen Rodgers
(b.1933)

◄ Alan Skilton
(b.1934)

Ruth Stanley
(b.1930)

Adrian Walker
(b.1938)

1942

Colin Ward
(b.1924)

Harriet Ward
(b.1930)

Index

The numbers in **bold type** refer to the figure numbers of the illustrations